SHIPS & SHORT SPLICES

SHIPS
&
SHORT SPLICES

George Gunn

GOMER

First Impression—2002

ISBN 1 85902 936 1

Printed in Wales at
Gomer Press, Llandysul, Ceredigion

To my wonderful wife, Betty,
who has kept ‘our ship’ on the correct course
through fair weather and foul, and on an even keel
while doing so.

P&Os popular passenger vessel *Uganda* berthed at Swansea awaiting departure on an Educational Cruise. *(Photo: Gareth Mills)*

CONTENTS

Preface 9

Foreword 11

CHAPTER 1: Glasgow & the Clyde 13

CHAPTER 2: Merchant Ships in War and Peace 25

CHAPTER 3: *Olynthus* & *Hong Siang* 57

CHAPTER 4: Sloan's: Deep-Sea to Coasting 70

CHAPTER 5: Bristol Channel Passenger Ships 75

CHAPTER 6: Bristol Channel Pilotage 92

CHAPTER 7: English Channel Ferries 94

CHAPTER 8: UK, Greece, Canada & Great Lakes 101

APPENDIX 1: Tramping as it was 119

APPENDIX 2: SS *Sheaf Holme* & The Longest Voyage 120

Foreword

I first got to know George Gunn when he was Mate of the White Funnel paddle steamer, *Cardiff Queen*, sailing from Swansea. I and a group of my teenage friends were regular passengers on those wonderful ships on many happy voyages in the Bristol Channel, mainly trading to North Devon and Lundy Island.

Indeed I am totally convinced by now that I am one of the passengers standing at the bow of the *Cardiff Queen* when the ship was approaching Ilfracombe pictured on the front cover of George's excellent book, *White Funnel Memories*. In his subsequent book, *Tramp Steamers at War*, he gave us a detailed insight into the hardships and dangers of being at sea in wartime in the Merchant Navy and the vital part these ships played in our country's survival and ultimate victory in 1945.

George's latest book, *Ships & Short Splices*, is a masterpiece of memory and history and highlights the old adage that no two vessels do things exactly the same way. This fascinating account of his experiences at sea is an important addition to the seafaring records of a nation which has for hundreds of years relied so heavily on people like him in both peace and war.

This is his third book of seagoing memories: we now have a trilogy, and all the books are written in an easy style and are full of personal anecdotes and humour.

I am delighted to be asked to write a foreword for this book, which will appeal to a wide readership, and I congratulate George on another success.

Commodore R. C. Hastie CBE RD* RNR
H.M. Lord Lieutenant of West Glamorgan.

Swansea Pilot Vessel *Seamark* – going on station on the 25th anniversary of service to the port in August 1984. *(Photo: Gareth Mills)*

Preface

My two previous books, *White Funnel Memories* and *Tramp Steamers at War*, accounted for about twenty of the fifty years I spent in the shipping industry. Sailing on ships in wartime and peacetime was an interesting and often exciting way to make a living and, in the '30s, '40s and '50s, it seemed the best course for a youngster to steer to get away from home, see the world, and, with a bit of luck, to have some kind of career ahead of him.

Glasgow and the Clyde housed the world's largest shipbuilders and was the home port of many major shipping companies, so with a war likely to start any day getting a ship looked easy. Engineers who had served their time in shipyards had few problems but nobody seemed to want deck cadets or apprentices. It took most of the first year of my war, walking around Glasgow knocking on doors and writing to shipping companies, before I landed an apprenticeship on a tramp steamer. Considering the huge losses during that year it seemed strange then, and even now, that there were so few vacancies for aspiring seamen like George Gunn, tailor's apprentice.

Since then, a lot of water has flowed down the River Clyde, and many changes have taken place both ashore and afloat. Most traditional practices and sayings have slipped through the net, but there are some which may still form part of a seaman's vocabulary from the old sailing ship days. 'Different ships – different short splices' is one of them, and was used for a number of reasons on all kinds of vessels: sometimes as a retort from one crew member to another who was moaning about something on board, saying, 'It wasn't like this on my last ship,' or to a 'sea lawyer' who knew everything but didn't want to do anything the way he was told to do it.

The ships and incidents written about here are drawn from just one person's varied career on land and sea. There were many ways of 'going to sea', many of which unfortunately are no longer available. This book is written with that in mind and hopefully will provide interesting reading to those who wish they had done so, and others who are sorry they did.

For help in obtaining material for this book I am indebted to:

Fotoflite for aerial photographs of ships
Gareth Mills for photographs of ships in dock
World Ship Society for Hogarth history
Imperial War Museum for naval photographs
John Greenwood's *Great Lakes Shipping*
Ships Monthly for permission to publish an article I wrote for the magazine
Bristol Museum for photographs of *Ettrick* in R. Avon
Mike Tedstone for photographs of *Waverley* and *Balmoral*

and also to my old shipmates and good friends,

Roger Whyte,
Nelson K. Harvey,
Bob Hastie,
Ken Sherrocks

for their personal contributions to the book.

George Gunn

Dowanhill Primary School. The boy sitting left of the centre with his arms crossed isn't happy.

CHAPTER 1

Glasgow & the Clyde

During the 1920s and '30s, the inner city of Glasgow had a reputation for poverty, deprivation and violence. Nevertheless, that reputation did not extend to the rest of the city and, despite the fact that I was born at 22, Gardner Street in Partick, and didn't know anyone during my earliest years who didn't live in a tenement building, little of all that was apparent to me.

When my family had arrived in Glasgow during the Great War they had all settled in the same part of the city. The women worked in the munitions while the men were sent to France. Granny Smith's trailblazing trek to the city in 1914 with seven children and no husband was followed by many other highlandmen for similar reasons: there was no money and no future in 'the back of beyond', and with 'a war on there was always hope of making a better living in the big town'. The remoteness of Ullapool and Stornoway, where they had lived off the land and out of the sea, later seemed to me to have been a more comfortable way to do it than trudging the unsympathetic pavements of Glasgow Corporation. However, after the Great War there were high hopes that victory would lead to a steady increase in economic prosperity throughout the country and where better to live in that case than in a large town or city? In Scotland it had to be Glasgow. Everything was promised, 'a land for heroes to live in, and the country's thanks for what they did', but that never came to pass. Shortly after I was born in 1923 the country was heading for its worst-ever depression. It was felt everywhere in the UK, but Glasgow, like New York in the USA, qualified as one of 'the biggest, the best, and the worst'. War sores and massive unemployment in the centre of the world's largest shipbuilding and ship repair industry quickly took their toll, and, like many other towns and cities in the Country, Glasgow slumped into the worst unemployment and living conditions ever suffered by most of its one million population.

At the age of 4, I was enrolled at Dowanhill Primary School, and was made to sit in the front row so that the teacher could keep her eye on me. Apparently it wasn't unknown for 'first dayers' to run back home. I took an immediate dislike to the place, as it was clear that my mother's disciplinary measures were very considerate compared to our teacher's. Playtime at 11 o'clock was the best part of my early education. In the three years that I spent at Dowanhill, I learned to play football and cricket, and when to fight or run when challenged. The wickets were chalked on the school wall and, despite the fact that he was an Australian, Don Bradman was everybody's hero.

A severe illness brought my primary education to a sudden halt, and most of my time was spent visiting the Western and Victoria Infirmaries, with a spell over Christmas as a patient in a Glasgow eye hospital. It all ended with an extended stay in the Western for a very delicate but successful head operation. Not long before this, my own mother had undergone the very same operation strapped to the operating table without any anaesthetic. The surgeon, Dr. Gavin Young did both jobs. Knowing what had happened to her, I gulped in too much gas and didn't come to until the following day. I woke to see a face peering down; it was Mr Riddle our headmaster; apparently I looked up and said, 'Who are you?', not a thing to say to headmasters in those days, but of course there were extenuating circumstances.

For fresh mountain air and a healthier climate I was sent to stay with my grandparents up in Ullapool in the north of Scotland to recuperate. My father had been born and brought up there, and at the age of 16 had left to join the Gordon Highlanders, knowing he was too young to be accepted. They were desperate for men, so he added a couple of years to his age and spent the rest of the war in France. He was discharged in 1919 with the rank of sergeant, stayed in Glasgow, found a job and married in 1922. He was killed by a bus on Dumbarton Road in 1926 coming home from work when his cycle tyre caught in tramlines. He left a widow and two children.

Ullapool was often described as the most beautiful village in Scotland. Apart from fishing-boats, the only access was via Inverness

The Gordon Highlanders in France. Private Roderick Gunn is on the far right.

to the railhead at Garve, then another thirty miles by solid-tyred stage coach on a rough twisting single-track road with passing places. Strangers going there had to have good reasons for doing so.

My grandparents' cottage at 7 Market Street had no drainage, electricity, gas, or running water. The pump was at the end of the street and one of my jobs was to fill enamel buckets with drinking water and galvanised ones for other domestic purposes. Water from the rain butts was used for washing clothes and satisfying the needs of two cows and other domestic animals. The gas lighting at home in Partick was more trouble and not as cosy in the winter as the oil lamps in Ullapool. Winters there were very severe and the only road from Garve was often impassable for as long as a week at a time. There was no mail, newspapers, or any other contact with the outside world. Marconi had successfully experimented with wireless transmission at the turn of the century, assisted by a Mr. Jamieson, who would later be my headmaster at Hyndland School in Glasgow, but it hadn't got very far north by 1931.

As in many other similar places, farming and fishing were the main occupations. When the horse and cart came round the streets filled with freshly landed herring, I was sent over with one of the galvanised buckets and a sixpence. The fisherman took the money and dipped the bucket into the herring until it spilled over the top. Fresh or salt herring was almost always available and very necessary at certain times of the year when other foodstuffs were in short supply.

The fishing and farming village of Ullapool had a profound effect on my education. Although my mother's family who lived in Glasgow could speak Gaelic it was never sufficiently spoken between them at home for us children to use it with any fluency or meaning. That altered after a few weeks at school and living with grandparents, who spoke nothing else unless it was absolutely necessary. I wasn't one of those necessities. A Sunday in Ullapool was very different from a Sunday in Glasgow: nothing that could wait until Monday was done on 'The Lord's Day'. It started with grace before breakfast and a reading from the Gaelic Bible afterwards by Grandfather; he and I then went off along Market Street to the Presbyterian Church a couple of hundred yards away for a two-hour Gaelic service, while Granny stayed home to cook the dinner. I went back from three until four for the Bible class, then home again for grace and tea. The three of us went back to the church from six until eight for a service in English. Before he went to bed, Grandfather would get out the 'good book' and read some chapters in Gaelic. In the summer it was all done in daylight; in winter, in the dark under lamps. There was no need of any tuition in trimming oil lamps when I eventually went off to sea as an apprentice in 1941. The shoes were all polished on Saturday, the dinner made ready to cook, and all the washing-up left until Monday. Apart from the Bible, the only book I was allowed to read was *Pilgrim's Progress* although Granny discovered I had got hold of a couple of comics, *The Skipper* and *The Hotspur*. She advised me to keep them under the mattress on my bed. They were still there when I left Ullapool to return home to Glasgow, where I stepped off the train at the Central Station carrying a bible and wanting to be a minister of religion.

The Boys' Brigade was founded by Sir William Smith in Glasgow in 1883, and in 1899 a similar body for younger lads was formed,

This picture of the sergeants of 51st Gordon Highlanders was taken in Germany. Sergeant Gunn is on the top right of the group.

original The Boys' Life Brigade, which united with the Boys' Brigade in 1926. Most meetings were in church halls, and Bible Classes on Sundays were a strict condition of membership. I joined the Brigade (known as the 'Lifeboys') in 1929, when the after-effects of a dreadful war were still very evident and the impression had to be given that it was not a military or political organisation. The fact that we drilled and marched around with rifles left over from the War didn't seem to cause problems or raise any objections.

Perhaps being a member of Sir William's 1st Lifeboys at the age of six and later joining the 5th Boys' Brigade at ten gave me a lifelong interest in the movement, which culminated some twenty years later when I was master of *Ravenswood* and we managed to pluck the members of the Newport BB Company and their camping kit off Weston Pier during a particularly strong gale in 1952 in the Bristol Channel. The presentation plaque still hangs in my office. Military training or not, the officers of the 5th B.B. had no problem qualifying for commissions in the Army; later most of them did return from Dunkirk. Colonel Scott, who sponsored and ran the 5th Boys' Brigade from his palatial home off Great Western Road, ensured that we were well trained, went regularly to Bible Classes, and attended annual camping trips if possible. He was a very nice gentleman, who, we understood, had an outstanding war record and probably wanted to make sure that his vast experience wasn't wasted on undeserving cases. It wasn't.

The annual camping trips combined arduous labour with enjoyment. Climbing over the Cairngorms in driving rain and then making camp at the end of a 'long day in the field' was just part of an exciting fourteen days under canvas. It was compensated for by a trip to Germany to have a look at the Hitler Youth Movement. Colonel Scott never spared anything, either money or himself.

While I was up North, the family had all deserted Partick and moved to new homes in Kelvinside, all within a few doors of one another. On my return, I was enrolled at my third school, Temple Primary, up from Anniesland Cross, and stayed there until I passed the qualifying examination for Hyndland Secondary. Changing schools so often in a short period of time didn't improve my interest in education. At that time school children in Scotland were force-fed with knowledge and had to learn whether they liked it or not. Penalties for open resistance were severe. The strap, or the belt, as we called it, wasn't spared, although age, sex and the degree of offence were taken into consideration. By the time I left Hyndland at fifteen I could clearly describe the straps used by every teacher at Temple Primary. They were all made of leather of differing lengths and thicknesses: some had thongs, or 'taws' as they were called, on the 'working end' (like a miniature 'cat of nine tails') and for security reasons they were usually locked up in the teacher's desk. Some who wore gowns in class carried their strap in one of the pockets with the outline clearly visible. There was little to remember about Temple except the convenient grassy patch near Anniesland Cross where we could play football or fight in comfort after school.

Ripon Drive, where we now lived, was one of three short residential streets situated in a small circular enclave with no real reason for anyone but the coalman, the milkman or the ashmen to drive round it on a daily basis. Periodic visits by workmen to the gasworks at the end of the street were one exception. We soon got used to the gasworks; little ever happened there and its unused piece of ground was handy for a bit of football in the summer evenings and other activities after dark during the winter.

The only way out from Ripon Drive was the way in past a football pitch with a small wooden changing-hut. I soon learned that the 5th Boys' Brigade regularly played there, and joined the 5th Company right away. Meetings were held at a nearby church up in Kelvindale and I remained a member until war started; then it was time to think of other things.

Hyndland Secondary was one of the largest and most successful local authority schools in Scotland. With about 2000 pupils, the sports and examination results compared more than favourably with any of the excellent grammar schools and colleges in and around Glasgow. The school had its own playing-fields at Scotstoun Showgrounds in Partick and lots of competitive sport was available but not guaranteed.

It depended on the amount of effort in the classroom, where there was much incentive to work hard and influence teachers, as the first opinions about a pupil's suitability came from them. It was sufficient motivation to generate a real interest on my part in education, and after one year I managed to keep getting more than the required 50% pass in all subjects except French. Miss Black, the teacher, had an alluring French accent and everything else to go with it. I didn't like the French language very much, and, as with Latin, thought it a waste of time, but I did like Miss Black.

In my third and last year at Hyndland, very much against tradition, I came top at French. Until then that had been the prerogative of the girls in the class: boys weren't supposed to be any good at languages. Perhaps talent sometimes lies dormant, waiting for the right incentive.

Although my Gaelic was seldom used and gradually forgotten, that can't be said for French. Without Miss Black's 'kick start' in the 1930s, I would not have been able to use the language effectively on so many occasions in later life.

During the '30s in our small community there were eight or ten boys of a similar age all growing up together, but we could never be accused of being members of a gang. Everyone had different interests, one being football and another riding bikes around the block. We all had one particular interest in common, Irene McCudden. The girls in Ripon, Kendal and Penrith Drives were outnumbered by boys by at

Queen Mary.

least four to one, so it didn't need raving beauty to stand out, but Irene would have done so whatever the odds. Giving the girls rides around the block on bicycle crossbars was the closest physical contact it was possible to make. I started at a disadvantage. Even if we could have afforded it, I was never allowed to own a bicycle because of the manner of my father's death, and had to be content with an occasional spin on someone else's, usually when there were no girls about. Irene was well protected by her family, having two experienced older sisters and her brother Frankie who was the current featherweight boxing champion of Scotland and the leading contender for a crack at the British title.

There were many changes between 1932, when I came back to Glasgow from Ullapool, and 1939, when the Second World War began. Glasgow itself never really changed, but things began to happen in the shipbuilding industry on the Clyde. Construction of RMS *Queen Mary* resumed after much delay due to the depression, and in 1934 the ship was eventually launched at John Brown's in Clydebank. We had time off school to wave to the King and Queen on their way along Great Western Road to the launch. Many fine ships had been built on the Clyde but none so significant as the *Mary*. It wasn't only that the largest and fastest passenger liner ever built was to be completed and put into service, but that hopefully it was the beginning of the end of almost a decade of mass unemployment and deprivation which had affected everyone in the country.

By the time *Queen Mary* made her maiden voyage in 1936 things had really begun to settle down, and the late '30s were easily the most enjoyable of my young life. Kelvinside and Anniesland were very different to Scotstoun and Partick, where the entrance to every tenement looked the same. There was more of a community outlook and even though there wasn't much more money around, there was great expectancy that something was about to happen.

Uncles, aunts, and cousins had joined the tribal surge from the city out west to Kelvinside and Anniesland; for all the years that had elapsed and all the wings that had been spread, Granny Smith was still in charge and always available for help and advice. In Stornoway, there had been no public transport: everyone either walked or didn't go at all. Granny Smith did not intend changing her lifestyle too much and flatly refused to travel with Glasgow Corporation. One trip on a tram was enough; she didn't trust them. The Gaelic Church on Highburgh Road was visited every Sunday, whatever the weather. Clutching the Bible, and with her flowerpot hat securely fastened with a six-inch pin to contend with all weathers, she walked there and back. Granny ruled all the family with love, affection, and a firm hand whatever their age; no one was ever known to answer her back. How times change!

After I started school at Hyndland, my life went through many changes, more than I should have thought possible in so short a period of time. Many formerly enjoyable things in life became mundane – for example, jumping on the back of the coalman's cart heavily loaded with bags marked 1/11½d cwt and with the 'coalie' coaxing his big awkward nag to put more effort into its tired legs to get up the hill towards the flat surfaces of Great Western Road. It was a dirty business for a joyrider, especially when it was raining heavily; on reflection it was difficult to remember where the joy had been.

And jumping off the tramcar without paying. It was usually a dare and quite a productive one, as I was given 2d a week to ensure that I got to school on time. A child's fare from Anniesland Cross to the top of Hyndland Road was a ha'penny, which wasn't bad even in those days for a mile journey on a tram. On Sundays the tram fare was a penny anywhere as long as you stayed on the same one. The best trip available for the money was 25 miles from Dalmuir West through the centre of the city and way out east from there. There were few stops for passengers on Sunday, and on long clear stretches trams proved why they were called 'rattlers'.

Secondary education and the fringe benefits of playing for one of the football teams made Hyndland much more enjoyable than any of my previous schools, but it took two of my last three years there for me to realise fully just how important it was to work hard as well as play hard; so instead of having the doubtful benefit of staying on for another year I had to be content with a lower instead of a higher leaving certificate.

Joining the ranks of the unemployed at the age of fifteen in a city like Glasgow was not the disheartening situation it might seem. Perhaps that was when my optimistic and confident approach to everything in life must have really started, and never stopped. Everywhere on the Clyde, prosperity or otherwise was directly dependent upon shipbuilding. Immediately after *Queen Mary* in 1936, an even larger Atlantic liner, to be named *Queen Elizabeth*, was being built at John Brown's in Clydebank, and was duly launched by our new Queen during the most settled period since before the First World War. As with the *Mary*, more than 250,000 people were at the launch, but unlike then they didn't see the ship leave the Clyde for Southampton to make her maiden trip across the Atlantic. Instead, *Elizabeth* quietly sailed light ship directly to New York to be fitted out for war service. During the next five years she made countless voyages all over the world as a troopship carrying more than 8,000 servicemen at a time.

In the '30s, Glasgow needed its picture houses, and there were lots to choose from. Chancellor Street, where we had previously lived, was ringed by them. At the top of Byres Road was the 'Hillhead' and, a short distance down from there, the 'Grosvenor', both charging three or four pence for a seat downstairs. A few hundred yards away on Dumbarton Road was the once famous 'Standard' where, at the age of six, I saw my first two films. They were silent except for a man sitting near the right-hand side of the screen, playing the piano. It is not too difficult to remember something about the films: the cowboy one starred Tom Mix and the other, Buster Keaton. The plots were probably as much of a mystery then as they are now. The 'Standard', for obvious reasons, was aptly called 'The Buggy' and was 'the cheapest place ever', to go to the pictures. A front seat on a wooden bench for a matinee was a penny. If any of them were not occupied by the time the programme started, then they were sold to those first in the queue waiting in the lane at the side of the cinema in exchange for a clean refundable lemonade bottle which was put into a large canvas sack hanging inside the back door to the lane.

Queen Elizabeth.

The next on the short clockwise circuit was the 'Western', where I saw my very first 'talkie'. It was *Ben Hur* and the cheapest seats there ranged from 3d to 4d. Further along Dumbarton Road was the 'Partick Cinema' then the 'Rosevale', where I watched the first Tarzan film, *Tarzan of the Apes*, starring Johnny Weissmuller. Just around the corner we came to the 'Tivoli', which installed double seats in the back row just when I was old enough to appreciate their use. They were a bit dearer but usually worth every penny.

The last of the nine cinemas on that two-mile walk around Partick and Hyndland was the new 'Ascot' at Anniesland Cross. We were watching a film there when the lights 'went up' for a speech by Winston Churchill. My pal who was with me at the time said afterwards, 'What a waste of time. It was only something about fighting on the beaches and in the fields.'

In addition to sport and the pictures, I was very interested in the wonders of radio and had managed to accumulate sufficient bits and pieces from various second-hand shops to build a one-valve short-wave set. By then we had a wireless at home that could only receive BBC broadcasts, so being able to listen to international stations, whether or not I understood them, was a great adventure at that time. The first English-speaking station I heard was from the USA, call sign W2XAD Schenectady, New York. A QSL card received from Warsaw Radio after I acknowledged a signal from them just before Poland was invaded by the Nazis was very exciting.

After leaving Hyndland it didn't take long to get a job; but unfortunately, despite the fact that I called at all the electrical and radio shops and distributors throughout the City I was unable to avoid being sent to the 'Burroo School'. Attendance at the 'Burroo school' was compulsory for boys who had left their own school and had no prospects of a job after two weeks. It was a strange place, but fortunately I was only there for a couple of days before starting work at Russell Moreland's Sports Emporium, which occupied a vulnerable position underneath the Central Station Bridge.

The job was described as 'apprentice salesman', but although I always turned up for work dressed in a blue serge suit, specially bought for the job, with a white shirt and my Hyndland School tie, I was never allowed to sell anything. The hours were eight to six during the week and nine to six on Saturdays. Shops in the centre of the city closed at 1.00 pm on Tuesday, and unless there was any extra (unpaid) work to do we had the rest of the day off.

Although there was no selling, there was plenty of other work to be done in and out of the premises. There were no cleaners employed, so that was one of the junior's jobs. Luckily, helping in the fields in Ullapool and doing other manual chores in response to Grandfather's constant order to 'make yourself generally useful, boy', had been good experience and conditioned me for work as an apprentice.

The six weeks that I spent at the sports shop were memorable in many ways. The first thing to remember was never again to work in a shop situated underneath the Central Station Bridge, especially if I had to do the cleaning. In order that prospective customers could see what was in the windows, the thick grime which had gathered overnight had to be cleaned off the outsides. That was always next on my itinerary after disposing of litter, empty bottles and a variety of other articles left over from the previous night's activities. The one part of the shop I quite enjoyed cleaning was the golf practice area down in the basement; there were always clubs and balls lying around needing to be tidied up. That was in 1938 and the first time I swung a golf club. In the last 60 years I have passed through many 'low and high waters' playing this game, but don't intend giving up just yet.

There was a continuous stream of tramcars passing under the bridge connecting almost every part of the city of Glasgow. Russell Moreland was a firm believer in personal service and sent most of his deliveries by courier. I was first in line for every job. The heaviest, though not always the most awkward, were cast-iron punchball bases; I rolled them across the road to the front of the tram and the tuppenny fare included the driver's help to lift them in beside him and to assist in getting them off and onto the pavement at the nearest stop to the destination.

It was a surprise when Russell Moreland made me redundant. If anything, I felt rather sorry for him that business was so bad it couldn't afford to support a payment of nine shillings a week or, to put it another way, less than two pence (2d) an hour. Prospects didn't look good, but it was only my first job and things were bound to get better. The real highlight of the six weeks was walking up Union Street carrying two well-packaged square boxes and wondering what passers-by would think if they knew what was in them. They were the gloves for the title fight at Shawfield Park between Benny Lynch, Glasgow's World Flyweight Champion, and Jackie Jurich of America.

Russell Moreland was a former professional footballer and then manager of Clyde, a yoyo kind of team too good for the Scottish Second Division but not good enough for the First, and consequently on the move from one to the other at the end of most soccer seasons. The team wore white shirts which put them and their supporters in the small neutral zone between the blue of Rangers and the green of Celtic. Where we lived almost everyone was a Rangers supporter and had been born and brought up in the belief that being protestant they had to follow the ''Gers'. Celtic followers on the other side of town were Catholics. It wasn't that they were fervent Christians, but there was never any better reason than religion to fuel the contention which has always prevailed in Glasgow and probably always will.

Attending football matches at Ibrox or Parkhead to watch Rangers and Celtic was no pastime for the faint-hearted nor for neutral supporters, unless they wore green or blue. Green at one end of the stadium and blue at the other. Two of us did go to Ibrox wearing our blue colours and deliberately went to the Celtic end and vociferously supported Rangers. We ended up having to take off the blue scarves, of course, and moved to another part of the terracing to make sure that we survived the rest of the game.

I watched my first New Year's Day Rangers and Celtic match at Ibrox Park when the weather was sunny, and it should have been cold, but there were too many spectators squeezed in to feel it. Ibrox Stadium was built to accommodate 120,000 but on that occasion they managed to get 128,000 into the ground. The mounted police outside and the ambulance men inside had a very busy afternoon. The ambulance men couldn't get to many of the large numbers of supporters who fainted, and throughout the game the crowd quickly and sportingly passed the 'bodies' overhead down to the front for revival. Of course, it had been Hogmanay just the night before.

The Labour Exchange sent me to R. W. Forsyth, and I was taken on as the kiltcutter's assistant at ten shillings a week, less the usual fourpence. Forsyth was the highest class store of its kind in Glasgow and was right opposite the Central Station at its main Gordon Street entrance. Although we employees had to queue up in the morning in the lane at the back to get in, it was clearly a step in the right direction. My blue serge suit, clean white shirt and Hyndland school tie stood me in good stead at the interview, and I was appointed as Mr. Archibald's one assistant in the important tartan outfitting department. We worked in a very small room right up at the top of the store, and although Mr. Archibald had no direct contact with customers and seldom saw anyone but me, he still wore the same as the other principals and floor-walkers – tails and striped trousers. My job was fetching the correct roll of tartan in accordance with the order, and after the kilts, trews and tartan jackets were cut, I carried the bundles across the lane to the girls working the sewing machines in an adjacent building. I learned all about Scottish tartans and a lot about girl machinists. At Christmas-time I doubled as a packer in the ladies' handbag department right in the centre of the shop. I couldn't believe what a rich person paid for just one handbag. My shyness didn't take long to subside; the salesgirls were very helpful and most considerate, but Christmas came round only once a year.

R. W. Forsyth was in a prime position right in the middle of everything in the centre of the city. It offered what was known as a 'dead men's shoes job'. All the senior staff had been with the firm most of their working lives and were dedicated servants of the company. I often called in the shop when at home on leave, but nothing ever seemed to change, and it was going to take more than a war to make it. I got all the latest news about the shop, but I sometimes wondered if they knew what was happening outside.

It is difficult to imagine a greater difference than that which distinguished Russell Moreland's sports shop under the Central Station

Bridge from R. W. Forsyth's Ladies' and Gents' Outfitters on Renfield Street. There were no discarded fish and chip remains (amongst other unpleasant substances) to scrape off the windows at eight o'clock every Monday morning. Luckily, takeaway curries hadn't reached Glasgow at that time. I really enjoyed every minute I spent working with different people in both shops: I couldn't get there early enough in the morning to start, and didn't care what time I finished.

A consolation gift from the senior sales in the sports shop was a pair of ice hockey boots and skates for half a crown. Working every Saturday temporarily scuppered my weekly football matches: in the morning it was Scotstoun Showgrounds, and in the afternoon the 5th BB at Anniesland. Friday night at Crossmyloof Ice Rink was a good alternative, where you watched an ice hockey match followed by general skating. I was well-prepared for life in Eastern Canada when we emigrated there in 1981. There everyone skated whatever their age, and, in accordance with the Constitution, whatever their colour, creed, or religion.

I spent one Hogmanay on the ice at Crossmyloof, where the few that were there skated round the rink holding hands and singing Auld Lang Syne. It was a bit disappointing, and I felt it would have been better to stay at home and take part in the traditional neighbourhood march around Ripon, Penrith and Kendal following Andrew McKay, the police constable, playing 'Auld Lang Syne' on the bagpipes to remind the other residents there that it was midnight.

My skating boots were used a great deal in both summer and winter, on ice rinks in summer and on ponds in the parks in winter. Bingham's Boating Pond on Great Western Road was near where we lived, and had the benefit of a covered area with a few seats to change boots, as well as another very important advantage: it was free. In Glasgow, ice skating in parks was free, and was, of course, a very popular sport.

Knowing that I wanted to be an apprentice of some kind, Mr Archibald advised tailoring and kindly recommended me to Thomson, Son & Wright, one of Glasgow's top-class bespoke tailors on Bath Street. They supplied liveries and other personal clothing for the residents and servants at Glamis Castle, the former home of Lady Elizabeth Bowes-Lyon, the Queen. They also made suits and coats for ship-owners and city businessmen at a price at least eight times the weekly wage of a qualified shipyard engineer.

The workroom was on the top floor of the building: tailors and their apprentices sat crosslegged on long benches with one foot on the floor and the other on top of the bench. A tailoress was always in attendance to machine up the long side-seams in jackets, coats and trousers. Apart from that, everything was handsewn. After a few days I was entrusted to join some bits of the material together with white cotton (known as basting), but my real job at the beginning was to make sure there was a continuous supply of fuel and to keep the stove at the end of the room in the correctly heated condition for the tailors' irons. Although I was apprenticed to one tailor in particular, Mr. Kennedy, I had a responsibility for everybody's pressing irons, but only fetched those required by Mr. Kennedy and Margaret, his tailoress. For different usages the irons had to be kept at various temperatures, and I sometimes wondered whether the expertise I acquired in guessing the heat of the iron by touching the handle or spitting on the surface of the iron itself would ever be of any use in a future career. After a few months I was allowed to do some serious sewing, and after a few more found that sitting crosslegged was more comfortable than any other position.

The War started, and the prospect of sitting on a wooden bench for the duration sewing up coats and jackets and waiting to be old enough for conscription didn't appeal, so I went along Sauchiehall Street to Lumley's Sports Shop as a salesman for 17/6d a week.

Lumley's Sports Emporium, Ladies' & Gents' Outfitters, another prestigious establishment, was situated at a prime location on the corner of Sauchiehall Street and Renfield Street. As could be expected, and as in R. W. Forsyth's, they also had well-established select premises on Princes Street in Edinburgh.

Lumley's stocked every bit of equipment and apparel that could be required for any sport in this country. My 17/6d a week was a huge pay rise and was a real incentive to work hard towards 'something', although at that time I was quite uncertain as to what exactly.

War with Germany was declared by Chamberlain in September, but up until the time I started with Lumley's nothing had really happened. The first winter of the war was one of the worst in living memory: I could put my ice boots on at home and skate on the frozen pavements to Bingham's Boating Pond half a mile away.

Because of my tailoring experience, I was given a salesman's job in the gentlemen's outfitting department up on the top floor of the shop and, because Mr. Scott the manager considered me to be very well qualified for the position, he increased my weekly wage by half a crown.

The War began to take off and the male staff took turns to stay up in twos all night twice a week on fire-watch duty. I was teamed with Jack McMinn, the resident golf professional, who was a former tournament player attached to the famous North Berwick Golf Club. The problems involved in staying awake all night were solved, therefore, with free golf lessons. These were the only golf lessons I ever had during sixty years' relentless pursuit of the game.

Underneath our shop was Lauder's Bar, one of the largest and best-known pubs in Glasgow. Our fire-watching covered their commitments and we were rewarded each evening with food and drinks. Food rationing was starting to bite, so anything extra, wherever it came from, was most welcome.

Apart from rationing, the blackout and call-ups for the forces, the war didn't really come home to Glasgow until the first heavy bombing raids by the Luftwaffe on Clydebank. Until then, things were going quite nicely. I had already decided that when eligible I wouldn't join the Army. Growing up in Partick, I heard and saw enough evidence from men who had been in the trenches in the First War to know there were better alternatives. Ernest hadn't yet invented the 'Bevin Boys' but if he had, that would have been the last option. There was still the RAF and the Royal Navy, and a combination of the two seemed to fit the bill, so I opted for the Fleet Air Arm. At the Naval recruiting office, because I was classed as a Boy, they could only sign me on for a minimum of twelve or twenty-one years. I was looking for somewhere to go for the duration, and as wars didn't usually last for more than five years I declined the offer.

Ken, one of my close friends, was studying to go to sea on merchant ships and he influenced me in that direction. He was doing a one-year cadet course at The Royal Technical College and was looking forward to a career in the Merchant Navy. It had always been his ambition, and during his year at college he was allowed to wear a smart officer's uniform with its little bits of gold braid. Wherever we went, Ken's tram fare was less than mine, and when we started to go to dances he always got off with the best looker. There seemed to be every incentive to follow him, so I enrolled at the Tech for a five-shilling night-school course in coastal navigation, to which I brought my own parallel rules, dividers, and a chart of Ardnamurchan Point to the Mull of Kintyre.

Lumley's was at the heart of Glasgow's theatres. Across the road from the shop was the 'Empire', around the corner the 'Pavilion', and within a few minutes' walk the 'Metropole', 'Kings' and 'Alhambra'. The theatres were convenient for access by members of the staff, and this was made much easier by the number of free passes Mr Scott handed out for allowing their notices to be exhibited.

My salary at Lumley's increased considerably, and this brought with it my first experience of independence and financial security. The way was opened up for golf at the Knightswood nine-hole course, easily accessible by tramcar for a penny each way and fourpence for the round of golf.

There was also an inclination to learn how to dance, as everyone I knew over the age of sixteen seemed to be going dancing somewhere. What we didn't know then was that, compared to other places, Glasgow was a Mecca for ballroom dancing. We found a suitable teaching studio on Great Western Road between George's Cross and Kelvinbridge. It was up the stairs in a close and nobody there would know us. Of course, when you strayed that distance away from home in Glasgow no one knew anybody. It was run by a very large man with a very small wife. They put on gramophone records and demonstrated what to do. We started with a waltz, the following week it was a quickstep, then a slow foxtrot and eventually we graduated to the tango. So for four shillings I learned how to dance, but not very well. However, as far as I was concerned it turned out to be the best thing that ever happened. I have been happily married for fifty-five years to one of the girls I met there.

During my travels around the world I often thanked the 'Elephant', as we called our teacher, for his patience and encouragement, which instilled sufficient confidence in me to go dancing at Seamen's Missions and other similar venues for lonely sailors ashore. Several holds were barred at Mission dances but there were lots of other places at home and abroad where the contact rules weren't quite so stringent.

When home on leave during the War there were always top-class bands which, because of air raid disturbances, had deserted London for Glasgow. They played at Green's Playhouse, the Locarno, Denniston Palais, Plaza and of course Shettleston Public Hall where one of my former Lumley colleagues played the saxophone. If you wore a uniform you had the advantage of not being asked 'are you C or P'? (Catholic or Protestant) before your invitation to dance was accepted by some.

For several weeks during the blackout I attended navigation classes at the Royal Technical College just off George Square in the centre of the city. All we did was chartwork, as most of the other students were studying for a yachtmaster's certificate, which, apart from basic seamanship, was all the knowledge required to sail around in small boats. I never wondered then why, during a war, these classes were run at all. Perhaps the fairly recent evacuation of thousands of troops from Dunkirk, where the little boats saved so many lives, may have influenced a decision to keep them going, as before 1938 Yachtmasters' Certificates were usually issued for leisure purposes. I never thought about that; at the time it seemed to be the only way to get to learn anything of any use connected with the sea. After reading a book entitled *Forty Years Before The Mast* I knew there was no alternative to getting away from Glasgow, putting on a uniform, and travelling around the world to ports like San Francisco or the Barbary Coast. I eventually got away dressed in a £2 MN cadet uniform jacket and trousers bought from an outfitter on Paisley Road West and although I sailed all over the world, I never did get to the Barbary Coast. The tailor personally presented me with a Merchant Navy Officer's cap and badge as part of his war effort.

In naval terms I was 'in all respects ready for sea' or at least I felt that way. The telegram arrived at Ripon Drive for me to go to Hogarth's office at 120 St. Vincent Street to sign the indentures, which required my mother's signature and some witnesses. It was easy to get witnesses' signatures but Mother held out until the very last before reluctantly agreeing. I read some of the clauses to her: she wasn't very impressed with the £50 the Company promised to pay me for the four years, but when we came to the bit about 'not being allowed to frequent taverns or alehouses and houses of ill repute' she thought that was 'all right anyway'.

CHAPTER 2 Merchant Ships in War and Peace

There could not have been a more dramatic start to the War for Scotland, and particularly for those of us living in Glasgow, than to read about the sinking of *Athenia*, which had sailed out from our city. Glasgow was considered the home port for *Athenia*, *Cameronia* and *Transylvania*, and all were well known, not only to grown-ups but also to countless children who visited the ships in organised school parties. We each had our own favourite ship. I liked all of them, but had been on board *Athenia* more often than the others. I had no intention then of going to sea, but I knew in my own mind that should it happen, *Athenia* was the kind of ship I'd want to sail on. It was difficult to believe unconfirmed reports that *Athenia* had been sunk, so I walked the four miles into town to read the grim notice shown outside the owner's offices near George Square.

The ship was torpedoed north-west of the Irish coast by U-30 commanded by Oberleutnant Fritz Lemp. His action in sinking a merchant ship without any warning was a flagrant violation of international law and was the cause of much condemnation from all over the world. It was said that Lemp did this against Hitler's orders, a statement with which very few agreed at the time and certainly nobody would believe now.

Apparently the Donaldson passenger vessel was advised by the Admiralty to steer well clear of the usual North Atlantic shipping routes, so it is likely that Lemp was quite surprised to meet *Athenia* in Latitude 56.44N Longitude 14.05W, 250 miles off Inishtrahull, Donegal. The ship was torpedoed in late evening on the day war was declared, 3rd September 1939, and was the first vessel lost. There were 1400 passengers and crew on board, more than 300 of them US citizens returning to America because of the prevailing crisis. Many stories of the sinking were published in the British and American press on the 5th of September, and understandably they varied considerably.

Torpedoing an unarmed merchant ship like *Athenia* was, of course, contrary to the international agreement signed as recently as 1936. By the 3rd of September, it was clear that the Nazis had no respect for agreements of any kind, ashore or afloat. The Prize Ordinance, as it was called, allowed attacks to take place on merchantmen proceeding under the escort of enemy warships or aircraft; merchant vessels which take part in any engagement, or which resist when called upon to submit to inspection; or troop transports which are deemed to be on active service, or belong to the armed forces and are to be treated as warships.

Because of the liner's unusual position, there seemed to be a slight possibility that U-30 mistakenly identified the darkened ship as a transport or AMC (armed merchant cruiser), both of which would have been lawful targets within the bounds of the Prize Ordinance. A decision to arm ordinary merchant ships sailing in convoys must have been a difficult one to judge at the time, as they then had no protection at all from any treaty. All British merchant ships were eventually fitted with four-inch or twelve-pounder guns and a variety of anti-aircraft weapons, from Lewis guns to Hotchkiss, and then twin Marlins. The PAC rocket launcher to deter Stukas and other dive-bombers was worked by pulling on a lanyard, usually from the protection of the ship's wheelhouse. This ejected a parachute tied on to 500 feet of wire with a Mills bomb on the end. The one time I saw this in action was when the Third Mate tripped over the lanyard when working on the navigation bridge. The sirens were sounded, and in minutes Kiddepor Dock in Calcutta was cleared in case the Japs were on their way. At the time, the ship was berthed there, loading cargo for Australia.

Apart from *Lusitania* and *Titanic*, more has been written about the fate of *Athenia* than any other vessel. *Lusitania* was torpedoed in May 1915 with the loss of 1198 lives. *Titanic* famously struck an iceberg in 1912 when 1600 were lost, and when *Athenia* was torpedoed in 1939, the total loss there was 112. The three ships had one particular thing in common: they were transatlantic passenger liners. As soon as was possible after the 3rd of September 1939, that type of ship was refitted and converted to either a troopship or an armed merchant cruiser. From a total of 14,439 on board troopships sunk by enemy action during the War, just 5,358 souls were rescued. Of the 805 lost on *Arandora Star*, 613 were German and Italian internees and there was only one survivor from the 650 on board *Ceramic*. Quite rightly, constant commemoration of the tragic and perhaps avoidable loss of *Titanic* is never far away, but we have to be reminded about *Lancastria* and *Laconia*, on which, between them, more than 5,000 service personnel and crew members perished. The sinking of *Athenia* signalled to everyone that a war really had started and the fine ship and her crew will always be remembered for that reason, if for no other.

* * *

During and between the two world wars, British merchant fleets were composed mainly of tramp steamers. These ships no longer exist, but for the seamen who sailed them they will never be forgotten. The steamers tramped around the world picking up cargoes of everything and anything, and loading and discharging anywhere it was possible to get to. The length of voyages varied from weeks to years, but for crews it was a case of 'the more days the more dollars'. The conditions on board also varied: none were good, and some were very much worse than others. Hugh Hogarth from Ayrshire in Scotland became one of the UK's largest trampship owners, established from a modest shipchandlers' and sailmakers' partnership in Ardrossan. Throughout an extensive building programme every Baron Boat, sail and steam, was registered in the port of Ardrossan. Their large fleet of tramp ships, which called at every seaport in the world, brought international recognition and trade to the area.

During the depression years, Hogarth was the only shipping company of its kind in the UK which didn't lay up a single vessel; in fact, their new building programme continued throughout. During the 1860s and '70s, Hugh Hogarth and his partner had operated a worldwide fleet of sailing ships, and after Captain Goodwin died, Hogarth moved the shipowning business to Glasgow. One of his young officers was a man named William Reardon Smith who joined the company as First Mate on the Mary Hogarth in 1878. This ship was a wooden barque built in 1875 in Canada. He went on to command several Hogarth sailing ships and took charge of the building of some new ships. Perhaps Captain Smith's most notable command was the famous *Machrihanish*. She was the company's first fully rigged sailing ship and one of the fastest afloat. Smith took her out on the maiden voyage and carried on as master on a number of the company's sailing ships and steamers.

Captain Smith's and Hugh Hogarth's last sailing ship was *Ochtertyre*; it was time then for them to get into the steamship business.

An order was placed with Turnbull of Whitby in 1881 and the first of many Baron Line ships was built and called *Baron Ardrossan*; not a surprising name, and one which was to prove very popular, as it was the first of seven *Baron Ardrossans* built for Hogarth. From then on every vessel had a 'Baron' prefix. They ran the ship for ten years and sold it to French owners.

In 1941, after knocking on every shipowner's door in Glasgow, I finally met with success at 120, St. Vincent Street, and was promised the next vacancy. Dunkirk had already taken place; Glasgow had just been bombed; the war was going on a bit and, not wishing to miss too much, I wanted to be off to sea as soon as possible. Until then, the only offer I had had was the one to sign on as a 'boy' in the Royal Navy. I had managed to get hold of an old copy of Lloyds List and had written to every shipowner shown on it. I received only one reply, from NYK Line saying all officers employed on their ships were Japanese. I didn't know until then that NYK meant Nippon Yusen Kaisha.

Two of the ships that Frank my stepfather had sailed on since the outbreak of war had been sunk, and he was at home recovering before going back to sea. The last torpedoing had been the worst, as he had sat in a lifeboat for several days with water up to the thwarts. At the

Baron Ardrossan I. Hogarth's first steamship, built in 1881, of iron, by Turnbull & Son of Whitby. Sold to France, 1891, and re-named *Emile*. Sold on to Rowe & Sons, Cardiff, and re-named *Baron Ardrossan*. Wrecked in 1898.

time I couldn't understand my mother's reluctance to sign my indentures. Frank said it would be all right to go to sea on merchant ships as long as it wasn't as an engineer and certainly not as a wireless operator. His support was much appreciated, and rather surprising, considering his own ordeals.

Frank declared himself fit to go back to sea. His London owners said one of their vessels was due in Glasgow from the USA and would be going from there around to the Tyne for convoy to Russia. I offered to go down to Yorkhill Docks and have a look at the ship on her arrival. I wasn't very impressed: she was loaded right down to her marks in a condition that I later learned to refer to as 'looking like a half-tide rock'. We suggested he declined to sign on in Glasgow and to ask the company if it was all right to join the ship in Newcastle, and they

Machrihanish, 1883. Hogarth's first fully-rigged ship.

Ochtertyre, 1885. Hogarth's last sailing ship.

agreed. His orders were changed and he was sent to another vessel. The first ship was torpedoed somewhere north of Scotland. Some years afterwards, during a discussion, an engineer on the ship I was on at the time said he had been one of very few survivors of the torpedoed vessel. He was lucky because the ship had a full cargo of high explosives. Frank was luckier: he didn't go on her at all.

Like most trampship owners in the days of sail and in the early days of steam, it didn't need torpedoes, bombs, or mines for them to lose ships. From the company's beginnings in 1870 until the outbreak of war in 1914 Hogarth operated a total of 33 cargo vessels and 28 of them were lost at sea by stranding, collision, fire and abandonment, or disappeared without trace for unexplained reasons. Between 1914 and 1918 a total of 18 ships were sunk by enemy action. Between the wars the company built up a fleet of 39 Baron Line steamers: 20 were war casualties, as were 12 others managed by Hogarth for the Ministry of War Transport. My visit to their office in St. Vincent

Street, Glasgow, started a career in shipping which lasted for more than fifty years. There was plenty of work for qualified, experienced deck officers anywhere in the world. Some started as deck-boys or apprentices and made their way up the ladder to become masters of the same company's ships. That was a routine life I didn't fancy, a fact which is unlikely to go unnoticed by readers of this book.

Tramping in war and tramping in peacetime were quite different. During wartime all British merchant ships were under the control of the Ministry of War Transport and operated world-wide in accordance with the national requirements at the time. However, general operations such as crewing, bunkering, storing, drydocking and repairs were still under the management of individual shipping companies, so there was little improvement in the conditions on board. The old sailing vessel 'pound and pint' which had been carried forward into pre-war steamer days was still working well for the owners into the 1939/45 War, but not for the crews on board the ships. The rather erroneous title, 'Merchant Navy', really referred to civilians who sailed on merchant ships in their accustomed civilian capacities. For most of them it was what they had been doing all their working lives and, having managed to get jobs on board ships during the depression and unemployment of the Thirties, they had no intention of giving them up. Instead of improving, mass living conditions in crowded fo'c's'tles, with sailors bunking on one side and firemen on the other, got worse instead of better as extra accommodation had to be found for naval and army gunners. Pre-war trampships were designed and built for the maximum stowage of cargo and the minimum carriage of everything else.

Wartime tramp steamer voyages under the Ministry were generally shorter than peacetime charters for the shipowner. The first priority then was to get foodstuffs and other essentials to the UK. This always meant convoy passages outward bound in light ballast condition and fully loaded on the return trip across the Atlantic. Oil tankers carrying high octane spirit and cargo ships loaded with explosives were given the safest possible stations in the middle of convoys. Although many made it because of that, others didn't.

I joined my first ship in July 1941 at James Watt Dock in Greenock. The *Baron Renfrew* was a flush-deck deep sea tramp built by D. & W. Henderson at Glasgow in 1935. Depending on the weather conditions, the quality of the coal, the firemen and the engineers, she could do anything between seven and ten knots on an economical consumption of twenty tons of fuel a day. The Baron Line was one of the largest owners of general cargo tramp ships sailing from British ports. For many reasons they were well known in all ports and places in the world where that class of vessel was likely to trade. They were also known as 'Hungry Hogarth'.

When I arrived at the ship she was in the final stages of discharging a full cargo of sugar loaded several weeks before at San Pedro de Macoris in the West Indies. In those days sugar cargoes were always lifted on board by ships's derricks in bags weighing about 200 lbs. and every inch of steel plating down the holds was covered with long lengths of timber before anything was stowed there. Reed matting was wound round vertical sections and after all that was completed the holds were considered sufficiently dunnaged to protect the cargo. After the war someone decided to load a full cargo of several thousand tons of sugar in bulk without any wooden dunnage or reed matting, and 4000 miles later, when it was unloaded in the UK, they found the sugar had suffered no ill effects. It must have been a blow to Hogarth, a company not renowned for unnecessary expenditure. Their vessels had in the past carried more sugar between West Indies and the UK than any others.

Leon C. Tessier and I arrived at the *Renfrew* together. Like me, he was on his first trip to sea and he had just finished a one-year cadet course at the Technical College. Theoretically, Leo knew what to do on board a ship and practically he knew how to speak about it in seamen's language. It was clear right from the start that my prior knowledge of chartwork would have to be put on ice for years to come as there were many more menial matters requiring attention.

After hauling our gear on board we reported to the senior apprentice in our new home. Bill had been on the *Renfrew* longer than anyone else and made us very welcome in the ten-foot-by-eight-foot

Renfrew gun crew, 1941: the four apprentices in 'action'.

cabin on the starboard afterend of the 'midship accommodation. He told us another apprentice would be joining the ship at Cardiff, where she was going to load for 'somewhere'. There were only three bunks and a five-foot-long settee between four of us, so it could be necessary to stake a claim to one of the bunks before the ship got to Cardiff. Priority depended on how long the other apprentice had been at sea and how tall he was. Leo was about six feet and I was only five foot six with no seatime at all, so it looked as if I would turn in curled up throughout my first trip to sea. So far I had never been used to the luxuries of life and having made it on board ship after such a long time spent trying to get the job, it was the least of my considerations. I just wanted to sail and get on with it.

Baron Renfrew, 1942. Sparks, two DEMS Gunners and one Apprentice.

The Mate took no time to make Leo and me realise why the Company had signed us on as apprentices. There was no crew on board, only a few local riggers and there was plenty to do to get the cargo finished, the holds cleaned out, and the ship made ready for sea. Everything was new, it was an exciting time, but things didn't look quite the same as they had on the pages of Nicholl's *Seamanship & Nautical Knowledge*. The worst time to look over a tramp steamer was during the final stages of discharging large homogenous cargoes, so there couldn't have been a better start to our seagoing careers.

A few nights ashore in Greenock dressed in uniform made us both feel like real sailors. Leo's was well worn after studying for a year at Captain Baldwin's navigation course in the Royal Technical College; mine required a gentle application of Cherry Blossom boot polish to tone down the giveaway lustre of the cap badge and the little bits of gold braid, which would surely have marked me out as a first-tripper.

Our first passage at sea started in Greenock, then we sailed across to Belfast to join a coastal convoy down the Irish Sea to the Bristol Channel, where the ship loaded a full cargo of military stores and equipment for the forces in the Middle East.

We joined a large deep-sea convoy and arrived at Freetown in West Africa four weeks later. Leading the column on our starboard side was *Windsor Castle* which, like all other vessels in the convoy, was painted dull Admiralty grey. Despite that, she was still a beautiful model of a ship, and it must have been frustrating for those on board to have to sail at less than half the speed of which she was capable in order to remain in the comparative safety of the nine-knot convoy. Like the *Renfrew*, many of the ships were taking much-needed equipment to North Africa; *Windsor Castle* was carrying thousands of troops who were even more urgently needed than equipment. At the time our army wasn't doing very well in the desert against Rommel. Cargo ships could get through the Canal, but although it was a risky business the troops were usually disembarked from the ship anchored off Suez.

Baron Douglas, 1945. Loading for home after the last convoy of the war.

Excluding Cardiff, my first foreign port was Freetown. It was the first of very many during the next four years of war. It was easy to grow up at sea on tramp ships and by the time it all ended in September 1945, I had sailed 137,000 miles on four Baron Line ships and had progressed to the position of Second Mate, with my apprentice days well astern but never out of sight. After enjoying three days of the novelty of West African heat, mangoes (before knowing they were from mosquito-infested mangrove swamps and carried malaria) and bargaining with bumboats, the *Renfrew* sailed south independently and arrived in Capetown on the 18th of September 1941, about six weeks after leaving Cardiff.

November 1942, ‘Operation Torch’. More than 500 British Naval and Merchant Navy ships on the way to the invasion of French North Africa.

Lamport & Holt vessel, *Delius*. This ship was right alongside *Yarborough* in convoy when it was hit on the bridge by Glider Bomb & all deck officers were killed except the Second Mate.

Italian cruiser *Barteloneo Calleoni* under fire from HMAS *Sydney*.

Outward bound, North Atlantic Convoy.

Barteloneo Calleoni, severely damaged and sinking.

Christmas Day 1941 in Indian Ocean.

There was no trouble spending the 10s. sub from the old man in two visits ashore. He didn't forget to remind us it was part of our combined £4 monthly good conduct money and war bonus, and there was little chance of any more for some time. After two years of blackouts, the lights all round Table Bay were an unforgettable sight. The passage from Freetown to South Africa had turned up everything we had read about and expected: warm sunny weather, the Doldrums, flying fish, albatrosses, learning how to steer the ship, chip and scrape rust off the decks and hatch coamings, and how to eat curry twice a day. We had signed on an Indian crew in Cardiff and from then on the smell of of curry was never far away. I had never seen it before, and really didn't like the look of it, but it took just a couple of months' self-induced deprivation to force me to eat it and enjoy it.

Before leaving Capetown, Leo and I went on board *Cameronia*. She was another of the Glasgow-based transatlantic liners we had known as schoolboys. She was on her way from Suez to the U.K. with Italian and German POWs, one of whom was a captured U-boat commander, whom we noticed got a bit of preferential treatment by being allowed to exercise by walking around the bridge deck, accompanied, of course, by a couple of armed guards. He must have been considered a prize catch as we understood all other POWs were safely locked up below.

The worst weather of the whole trip was between Capetown and Durban when the ship was hove to for three days in a strong gale and took six to get there. We only bunkered and stored in Durban but one night ashore was enough to look forward to getting back there again. Apparently the ship's agent told the old man the following day that a group of sailors had taken a car the night before and freewheeled down a hill in it. I couldn't tell a lie when asked by the Mate about it, and said, 'I didn't freewheel down a hill in a car last night sir, I had to stand outside on the running-board.'

The ship arrived at Aden 14 days and 3000 miles after leaving Durban. We were once again in bumboat territory, but it was a little more sophisticated than at Freetown. They were selling Gold Flake and Capstan cigarettes at less than half the old man's duty-free price.

Baron Renfrew.

Although the packets looked exactly the same, my more experienced colleagues said they were fakes.

We spent two days at anchor off Aden, then set off up the Red Sea to Suez. We didn't know then that the Luftwaffe had been targeting troopships there when the vessels were disembarking their cargoes of servicemen. A very recent casualty was the *Georgic*, which had been heavily bombed, set on fire and was lying on her side abandoned in the Bay.

After transiting the Canal we berthed in Port Said to unload some of the cargo. The bumboat men at Port Said were efficient at their work and well known to every British seaman whose ship called at the port. They seemed to be free to go on ships and bring on board anything required by members of the crew, and could make arrangements for anything they wanted ashore, including a boat and ghari to get there. The Empire Theatre in Glasgow was the first 'Palace of Arts' I had ever visited; the 'Golden House' in Port Said was the second one. They were very different experiences. The 'Golden House' prospered for about another year before British and Australian troops on their way to Alamein and the Western Desert said their fond farewells, then burned it down. Their reasons for doing so went west with them.

In addition to one trip to the Golden House with the DEMS gunners, another memorable occasion ashore that time was a guided visit by an Arab urchin to the Port Said Cinema. I sat on a backless wooden form (similar to the old 'Standard' picture-house in Partick) squeezed in between two Arabs, and watched their presentation of *The Great Dictator*. Each sequence was either applauded or booed. The film was in English with French subtitles, and down one side of the screen there was Arabic and down the other side, Greek. None were synchronised and, as a result, everyone laughed at the jokes or shouted at Hitler or Mussolini at different times.

Georgic.

The next port was Haifa in Palestine to discharge the rest of the cargo. Although the dockers worked around the clock, it took two weeks to unload everything, which gave all of us time to get to know a bit about Haifa and Palestine. Jews and Arabs didn't mix and seemed at that time to tolerate each other and to go about their own business.

Haifa cinemas and cafes were very attractive to seamen: during the show they served hot corn on the cob and cold fresh orange juice, and the mainly Jewish audience was very quiet.

When we came back aboard from the cinema one evening a warship had berthed on the opposite side of the quay. By the time we turned to in the morning it had sailed. Bill had been on nightwatch and said the ship had only come in to Haifa for bunkers, stores and water, and one of the crew told him her name was *Sydney* and they had sunk an Italian light cruiser, the fastest one in the world.

From Haifa our next port was Bombay in India. It took sixteen days and about 4000 miles and we arrived there on the 28th of November. Apart from our other sailoring duties during the passage we had gun practices every day. Captain T. R. (Tommy) Reid had served in the Navy in the first War and ensured our six DEMS gunners, and we four apprentices, knew what to do if an emergency arose. Sailing independently out of convoy was the only circumstance in which it was possible to have gunnery practice at sea, and Captain Reid, or 'TR' as we called him, took full advantage of it. Whilst the northern areas of the Indian Ocean were considered to be enemy-free zones, there was always the possibility of a chance encounter. We knew that was the worst possible scenario for a merchant ship, but nobody ever spoke about it. Three weeks later, on the 6th of December, all that changed: the Japanese bombed Pearl Harbour, and from then on the Indian Ocean was another dangerous area for British shipping.

Another memorable occasion on my first trip was at daybreak one morning off Perim Island at the southern end of the Red Sea. I was at the wheel on the First Mate's watch when what looked like masthead lights showed ahead, coming up very fast. It was *Queen Mary* & *Queen Elizabeth*, fully loaded with Anzac troops for Suez. Our close proximity and the wash from both vessels gave the *Renfrew* the heaviest roll we had experienced since the Cape of Good Hope.

As the ship only had sufficient stores for the normal passage from Bombay to Durban and had to return to port because of Pearl Harbour, Christmas Day in the workhouse was never as frugal as the 25th December, 1941, on board the *Baron Renfrew* in the middle of the Indian Ocean. A small 'celebration' sherry each and a 'Merry Christmas' greeting from TR was followed by single rations of the contents of a barrel of 'salt horse', a large spoonful of haricot beans and one potato. The old man assured us the meat tasted like chicken. We looked forward to Durban and something to eat.

A full Lascar crew change took place in Bombay. The problem of continually drinking warm water from our daily ration pumped up from the ship's two eleven-ton steel domestic tanks was slightly alleviated after buying a couple of 'chattys' there. These were thick, crude, rather porous earthenware jugs which could be suspended in an alleyway, either up on the boat deck or anywhere that a cooling breeze was likely to be generated, however slowly, from the ship's movement through the water. At that time refrigerators of any kind were unheard of on most tramp steamers.

The ship arrived in Durban on New Year's Eve and spent the next week loading consumable cargo destined for the UK, an especially enjoyable task for us, as we knew how bad the food situation was at home. Durban hospitality to seamen ashore and to servicemen on their way to the Middle East was renowned throughout the War. Bobby, the apprentice who joined the ship in Cardiff, was taken ashore sick and the ship left Durban without him.

Our next port of call was Freetown for a homeward-bound convoy, and we arrived back in Hull safe and sound on the 24th of February, 1942. During the seven-month voyage, and unbeknown to us then, 357 other British merchant ships weren't so lucky, and had been lost to enemy action.

My second trip on the *Renfrew* was the longest, the best and the most interesting of all. After upgrading the ship's defence and lifesaving gear by changing old Oerlikon guns with not quite so old Marlins, and adding water-distilling machines for the lifeboats and large crates of patent fuel to get them going, the ship was in all respects ready for sea, and left Hull on the 12th of March for what was supposed to be a short trip across the Western Ocean to the States and back. One year later we were on our way back across the Atlantic to the UK after a complete circumnavigation of the world, having sailed through every war zone in the East and West. From Hull it was one coastal convoy around to Loch Ewe in Scotland to join another Atlantic convoy across to the States. From Baltimore we sailed independently down to Capetown, then to Basra, where we discharged a full cargo of army stores and equipment including crated fighter aircraft for the forces in the Middle East. We then called at Abadan, where I was taken ashore to hospital with dysentery and spent several days recovering in the luxury of a clean, comfortable bed with air-conditioning controlled at 65-70 degrees. The ship sailed without me, but after three weeks working in the stifling 120+ degrees at Basra I was sorry to be discharged from the hospital and put on board a similar ship with the same range of facilities as the *Renfrew*, except that the officers got a small daily ration of cold water from a fridge.

My subsequent DBS trip across India from Karachi coincided with Gandhi being gaoled by the British, which resulted in thousands of his supporters tearing up the railway lines between Karachi and Calcutta where, eventually, I was very relieved to rejoin the *Renfrew*. I had been assured in Karachi that under the existing conditions there was no way across India to Calcutta and was advised to try, if possible, to get a ship back home. 'TR' had paid me off in Abadan and had not expected to see me again, but I surprised him and the agent by turning up at Calcutta Shipping office just as they were signing on a new Indian crew before the vessel sailed.

After changing Lascar crews, the ship sailed for Australia. By then, Japanese success in Malaya and Burma had brought the war closer to India, which caused great concern in Calcutta. There were chaotic scenes as men actually fought each other to get a job on the ship – usually white deck and engine crews did everything they could to avoid having to sign on Baron boats. Our complement was thirty-five Lascars and about fifteen others depending on the number of DEMS gunners put on board by the Navy.

The passage from Calcutta to Freemantle took about three weeks. By then German and Japanese subs and surface raiders were well established in the eastern part of the Indian Ocean, and the ship's courses which were independently routed to Western Australia had to pass uncomfortably close to Burma, Malaya and the Dutch East Indies. Freemantle/Perth, then Melbourne, Sydney and Newcastle NSW proved to be the best part of the voyage, and it was further enhanced by the fact that John Ellerby, one of the apprentices, jumped ship in Newcastle, which relieved the pressure of our cramped living conditions in the ten-by-eight cabin. Although it meant doing watches of four hours on and four off, as well as field days for the rest of the trip, it was well worth the extra work; we also made sure that the immigration people wouldn't catch him by giving them a photograph of someone else.

The ship loaded a full cargo of coal in Newcastle for Montevideo in Uruguay, and after sailing more than 9,000 miles we arrived there on the 24th of November without seeing any other ships, much to everyone's relief. In Newcastle, TR was warned against going through the Magellan Straits because of submarine activity there, so we went round Cape Horn.

We were in Montevideo for ten days discharging the coal and getting the holds cleaned up to load grain.

The 4500 miles up the east coast of South America to the West Indies passed without incident, although TR seemed to make many alterations of course far out into the Atlantic. At least that was what it looked like: with pre-war masters like Captain Reid, officers were discouraged from divulging such information to members of the crew, including apprentices. Most of our information at sea was obtained from the radio operators, who picked up distress calls in Morse from ships in trouble. On this particular journey, calls became much more frequent the nearer the ship got to the Caribbean.

We arrived in Trinidad on New Year's Day and the amount of U-boat activity around there was evident from the large numbers of survivors ashore waiting for ships to take them back to the UK. We took three of them: for the first time we definitely knew the *Renfrew* was homeward bound, but we still had about 5,000 miles to go.

From Trinidad we went to Guantanamo in Cuba for convoy to New York. Guantanamo was an American naval base and they had recently started running convoys to and from there, something everyone but Admiral King in charge of US Naval operations thought should have been organised long before, and which would have resulted in a much reduced loss of Allied ships sailing up and down the US coast to join North Atlantic convoys across to Britain.

Another loss that could have been avoided was that of the five teeth that I had extracted by a resident US Navy dentist at Guantanamo. He got so carried away telling me about all the wonderful times he had had in Scotland before coming out to Cuba, and how much he had enjoyed Glasgow and the 'beautiful broads', that he forgot to stop pulling until it was too late. I reckoned the nett loss was three teeth and I bled all the way up to New York. We had only two nights there before we joined an eighteen-day convoy across the Western Ocean to Loch Ewe and a coastal one around the north of Scotland, where we anchored off Leith. We berthed and discharged the grain cargo and from there we headed down to the Tyne for drydock. The estimated steaming distance for the trip was more than 47,000 miles.

I did one more trip on *Renfrew* over to the States, then down to the West Indies for a cargo of sugar. TR signed off the ship and went home to Leith for a well-earned break. I, for one, was sorry to see him go. He was a strict disciplinarian but highly respected by the officers and crews we had carried during the eighteen months since the ship first sailed from Cardiff in 1941. In that time we had three different Lascar crews, several changes in deck officers, engineers and wireless operators and especially DEMS naval gunners who were put on board or transferred to other ships anywhere and everywhere we were likely to dock. The *Renfrew*'s average complement was thirty-five Indians and thirty others.

I was more than sorry to see Fred Davis and Bill McLennon, two of our gunners, leave in Leith as by that time I had sailed with them through thick and thin. Fred, the gunlayer from Battersea in London, was in charge and described himself as a 'high class barrowboy'. Bill was a hard, tough Newfoundlander (weren't they all?) who ran his own taxicab service before being called up for the Canadian forces. Fred taught us how to try to defend ourselves at sea with the limited armament available on the ship. He also showed us on several occasions how to defend ourselves ashore against the odds. After a year and a half spent living and working in close confinement and in the extreme conditions on board these ships during the War, it didn't take long to get to know who you could rely on. Although it was never ever spoken about, I'm sure others, like myself, decided quietly upon whom we would prefer as companions in a lifeboat or on a raft. Bill was top of my list, ashore or afloat.

I had a week's leave in Glasgow and enjoyed every minute of it, but as before, despite everything, I was glad to get back aboard the ship and looked forward to sailing on the next trip.

South Shields was almost a home port for Baron boats: the ships were too well known, and it wasn't always easy to get good men to sign on at Mill Dam shipping office. The ship spent almost a month being refitted at Brigham & Cowans shipyard before we sailed round to Scotland in convoy, to join another convoy across the Western Ocean to Halifax. From Halifax the ship went down to Brooklyn, New York, to load general cargo on a US charter for the West Indies. We were two weeks loading in Brooklyn, and by the time the ship sailed, there was little we didn't know about New York City. It was a fabulous place in those days; the British pound was set for the duration of the War at a minimum four dollars & four cents. A beer or a pack of cigarettes was ten cents; it cost only ten cents to go anywhere on the underground as long as you stayed down there. By then I was a senior apprentice and although it was an honorary position it was the first time I had ever been promoted to anything. I felt then more like a sailor and less like an 'apprentice boy'; (to be 'taught the business of a seaman' was all Hogarth had agreed to in my indentures). How to become a ship's officer was my own business

SS *Baron Yarborough.*

We sailed from New York in another American convoy down to Guantanamo in Cuba. Luckily, the teeth the US Navy dentist had left me with from our last visit there were in good condition. Even if they hadn't been, it could have been preferable to wait until the ship docked at Ciudad Trujillo in the lawless republic of Haiti, where seamen were advised not to wander around on their own at night. However, every provision was made for everyone's comfort and entertainment at a number of very convenient 'drinky-dancey' joints just across from where the ship was taking on board the part cargo of sugar. We spent eight days down the holds dunnaging the bags at Trujillo and eight doing the same at another 'Pearl of the Caribbean', Barahona, where we loaded the rest of the cargo, then sailed to Guantanamo to join another American convoy up to New York.

By the time we left New York I had decided to ask for some leave and a transfer to another ship. The new captain was very different to TR and although we weren't always clean and tidy he treated apprentices like dirt. That seemed a good reason for getting out and going elsewhere if possible, and two years on the same ship during the war seemed long enough for leave and consideration for transfer. I was on my best behaviour throughout our short stay in New York, and all the way home through Long Island Sound, the Cape Cod Canal to Boston, then Halifax for convoy across to Loch Ewe, and coastal convoys from there round to Methil, then down to London to discharge the sugar. Unfortunately, when we got there, the dockers went on strike because the bags were too heavy for two men to lift. It had taken just one to lift them when loading in Cuidad Trujillo and Barahona. In July 1943 food shortages were at their worst, and 5,000 tons of sugar was sufficient for at least a week's ration for everyone in Britain. Churchill sent in the army and the whole cargo was discharged, the holds cleaned out and the ship was made ready in three days to leave London to load elsewhere.

My request for leave was successful and I had two weeks at home in Glasgow before joining another vessel in Greenock.

My next ship was *Baron Yarborough*. We sailed from Greenock on the 20th of August 1943 to load a cargo of coal in Cardiff. Built in 1928, she looked every one of her ten years older than the *Renfrew*. So far the *Yarborough* had come through the War unscathed, but that wasn't apparent to anyone looking at her alongside the quay in Greenock. By the time the ship was full of coal and we were due to sail from Cardiff she looked like the proverbial 'halftide rock', and I couldn't imagine her being able to make enough speed for a nine-knot convoy. The officers on watch had to work hard to keep her there, but it was only a short passage as far as Gibraltar, and then we travelled on independently from there to Bizerta in North Africa.

My three months on the *Yarborough* were far more exciting and interesting than any during the War, and we were pleased to get back to Ardrossan after our homeward-bound convoy was dismantled by U-boats, dive-bombed, and attacked by radio-controlled glider bombs, which no one had ever seen or heard about before.

It is my impression that the *Yarborough* survived because she was the scruffiest-looking ship in the convoy, and selective bombing by Heinkel aircraft using radio-controlled glider bombs gave them the opportunity to choose any target they wished, the bigger the better. As she was fully loaded with copper ore, there wasn't much of the *Yarborough* showing above the waterline. After dodging around the Mediterranean before discharging the first cargo in Sicily, we ran out of edible stores, and when we did get to Huelva, we spent our one night ashore running away from members of Franco's Blue Brigade on leave from the Russian front. We weren't forewarned about these men; when they were on leave they dressed in civvies and spent their furlough in the sunny south of Spain and further enjoyed themselves beating up British seamen ashore in the Port. One night there was enough.

All the crew would have jumped ship if there had been anywhere to go, but we had to content ourselves with moaning, groaning, getting drunk when possible and threatening mutiny. Nobody signed on for the next trip; and that included the senior apprentice.

My next ship was the *Baron Forbes*: built in 1915, she was a German prize from the First World War and had been on a regular service between Glasgow, Lisbon and Huelva since she had been

Baron Yarborough. Heavy weather in the North Atlantic.

taken over in the early '20s by Hogarth. She was the best-known foreign-going vessel trading from Glasgow, with the best-known senior officers. Between them the master, chief and second engineer had sailed on the ship for a total of forty years. Their reluctance to go anywhere else was understandable: they were only ever away for a few weeks at a time, with long periods spent in their home port loading and discharging general cargo. I was sent there because there was only a short time to go before I had sufficient sea-time to sit for a Second Mate's certificate.

I thought the *Forbes* would be the oldest vessel I was ever likely to sail on. It didn't turn out to be the case, as much later in my career it was bettered by one built in 1891 and another in 1896. After all the years that she had trudged during peacetime and wartime up and down between Scotland and Portugal, this was to be the *Forbes'* last voyage on that run. It was my first and I couldn't understand how this little ship had managed to sail back and forward through one of the most dangerous areas in the North Atlantic for so long and stay afloat. She couldn't do more than about eight knots under favourable conditions, and being left behind by a convoy was a perilous plight for any ship to find itself in, particularly during the early years of the war. She sailed independently to Huelva and Lisbon after her convoy dispersed at Gibraltar and was again on her own after leaving the

Baron Yarborough in the Bay of Biscay in particularly bad weather.

loading ports and was sailing right out into the Atlantic where they hoped to pick up a homeward bound convoy to the UK. I kept wondering how the old ship got away with it, as she had been doing that for four years since war started in 1939. Huelva and Lisbon were well covered by German agents. From Algeciras every ship movement at Gibraltar was easily observed and Allied ships were sunk by limpet mines with the full approval of the onlooking Spaniards. So much for neutrality!

The *Forbes* carried two of us apprentices.The other one, Dave, had been on the ship for more than two years and was well into his sea-time for a Second Mate's ticket. The only ports he had been to during that time were Glasgow, Lisbon and Huelva. Under strict security in Glasgow we loaded a full cargo hold of Scotch Whisky and discharged it in Lisbon under even greater security. According to Dave 'the ship carried her own insurance' as he had seen large consignments of the whisky being discharged from the holds straight into railway trucks marked 'Hamburg'.

By the time I arrived there in 1943 it looked as if we were beginning to win the war, and many known German agents were being sent home by the Portuguese, though not by Spain. There were still many operating openly in Lisbon, which in a strange way made it one of the more interesting ports I had been to since going to sea.

I asked Dave what he meant by 'carrying our own insurance', and he said that on a previous trip a German plane had flown over, had a really good look at the ship, flown away and attacked another vessel; the *Forbes* was well known to them and the Germans didn't intend to cut off their only guaranteed supply of Scotch. It is difficult to believe now that Captain Lachie McPhail, the master of the *Baron Forbes*, didn't know then that he was helping to supply the German High Command with Scotch Whisky. However, he made amends by taking part in one of the most important and successful military coups of the war, one which helped save the lives of countless Allied troops during the Sicily landings. The whole story is told in *The Man Who Never Was* by Ewen Montagu, the architect of the scheme.

After almost three weeks in port working cargo we sailed from Lisbon via Gibraltar for convoy to the UK. The whisky discharged in Portugal was partly compensated for by loading large wooden butts of port and sherry containing more than 100 gallons each.

We left Lisbon on the 5th of April and picked up a homeward-bound convoy off Gibraltar to Loch Ewe, then joined a coastal convoy round the north of Scotland down to Leith and on to the Tyne to discharge the cargo and sign off the crew.

Third Mate, *Baron Forbes*.

New articles were opened at Mill Dam shipping office in South Shields: Lachie promoted me and I was signed on as Third Mate and we sailed from the Tyne in another coastal convoy back to Loch Ewe for a North Atlantic convoy across to the States. The *Forbes* had never sailed across the Atlantic or done anything like 3,000 miles at one go. Even I, a green young Third Mate, knew the old ship could never maintain enough steam to keep up with a nine-knot convoy in the Western Ocean for at least three weeks. For me it was an exciting thought; for Lachie and his other two experienced Mates it was a worrisome time. Like many of the older prewar tramp steamer masters, Lachie McPhail didn't like convoys and couldn't stand Royal Navy escorts telling him what to do with his ship – although he wasn't averse to telling them what to do with theirs.

Our crew troubles started immediately the ship left the Tyne, with firemen who couldn't raise steam and a cook who couldn't cook. Lachie got rid of all the firemen at Loche Ewe, and after three days trying to eat the cook's lumpy porridge he fired him as well. Although I had been brought up on porridge I lost the taste for it once and for all on the *Forbes*. An inspection of the galley showed that some of the lumps were cockroaches which fell from the hot deckhead above into the large open pot simmering invitingly on top of the coal-fired stove.

Little else that he cooked was edible, not even the currant buns he made as a special treat. We threw them over the side to the seagulls but they were so heavy the birds couldn't pick them up off the water.

Nothing was routine about keeping bridge watch on the *Baron Forbes* in convoy. It was challenging and interesting. By the time I became Third Mate I had plenty of experience of steering ships, doing what I was told, and sometimes questioning in my mind why I was ordered to do so. After a couple of watches on the bridge on my own trying to keep the old ship on station in convoy, I am sure the man at the wheel must have had similar feelings. Like most Third Mates on cargo ships I kept the 8-to-12 watch morning and night. These were the most convenient times for the old man to keep his eye on the least qualified and experienced watchkeeper without losing much sleep. At the beginning I had Lachie's company for fairly long periods, but even with him there it wasn't possible to keep up with the other ships.

The convoy eventually left us behind three days before we were due in New York. After more than two weeks spent cajoling the ship, fighting with the engineers and cursing the firemen, that wasn't too bad a result. That situation a year earlier in the same position in the North Atlantic would almost certainly have spelled disaster for us.

We never managed to get into station on the next convoy from New York bound for the West Indies. When I went off watch at midnight we were trying to catch up with the rest of the ships, and when I came back on the bridge at eight in the morning they had all gone. We made Key West after sailing close inshore right down the US coast, and eventually got to Georgetown, British Guyana to load sugar for the UK. After several weeks spent sailing around the West Indies and another three berthed at the foot of 33rd Street in Manhattan waiting to be accepted by a convoy slow enough to take us back across the Atlantic, we sailed from New York and arrived in Liverpool on the 18th of August 1944. Having volunteered to go on a ship for the D-day Landings in Europe, it was disappointing to know that it had all taken place when we were sculling around the West Indies on the *Forbes*. There was little doubt as to why our ship had been sent well away from Europe.

Although an apprentice was indentured to a shipping company for four years, this didn't necessarily mean that he had to stay there that long. The amount of seatime on ships' articles was the criterion for sitting a Second Mate's certificate. I had accumulated enough by the time I signed off the articles at Liverpool in August 1944, exactly three years after my first trip. Three and a half months as Third Mate on the *Forbes* at £17 10s. a month plus War Bonus and Indenture Money helped me to live at home and study for my Second Mate's certificate at the Royal Technical College. I passed the exam in December and joined the *Baron Douglas* at the Tyne in January.

Captain Blackwood was Master of the *Douglas* when I first went there. He told me to sign on a full crew at Mill Dam Shipping Office in South Shields on Friday, with the ship due to sail Monday. He would be back in Newcastle on Monday morning in time to take her away and expected everything to be 'shipshape and Bristol fashion'. There was no trouble signing on the officers, deck hands and stewards, but although the firemen had been sent from the Seamen's Union they didn't want to go on the ship. We managed to persuade some to do so but it looked as if there would be crew trouble before too long. Unexpectedly, there wasn't, on that trip. The ship loaded at Hull for Sète in the South of France and arrived there a short time after it was vacated by the German Army. The place was badly bombed and the people we met ashore hadn't quite recovered from the occupation. Reprisals against collaborators seemed to be gathering pace: for example, one girl in a cafe said to us about another, 'She no good she go with Boche.' Although we didn't know then, it turned out to be free haircuts all round.

We said goodbye and best wishes to the cafe proprietor, his wife and clientele and were moved by his response. He said that it was the first time in years that visitors had spoken to them in anything but German.

The *Baron Douglas* sailed from Sète on the 10th of March to Gibraltar, and on to Takoradi on the Gold Coast to load a cargo of ore for London. I was then well established as the navigating officer, although Blackwood wasn't the kind of person to trust anyone's judgment but his own. He was very impulsive, quite a good shipmaster but not too easy to satisfy; he had been in charge of the *Renfrew* when, just before I joined in 1941, she was abandoned in the North Atlantic after an unexploded bomb was discovered in one of the holds.

After discharging in London, the vessel went up to the Tyne and as we entered between the piers, every ship in the port and river and everything which had a whistle or foghorn or anything else that could make a noise, sounded it joyously. We guessed it wasn't our arrival that prompted this ecstatic welcome; it happened to be 5.00 p.m. on the 7th of May 1945 and the end of the war with Germany. It was another unforgettable occasion.

After a week in the Tyne we sailed on our last North Atlantic convoy, bound for Newfoundland. The convoy was dispersed three

Baron Douglas, ashore following a post-war refit.

days before our arrival there, and we were told to continue independently to wherever we were going. It was the final Western Ocean convoy of the war, and I would have liked to have been standing beside Lachie on the bridge of the *Forbes* instead of Blackwood on the *Douglas* when the signal was received from the Commodore Ship. Whatever Lachie had to say about convoys, commodores and the Royal Navy would have been worth remembering.

We spent several weeks at logging camps and various other places we had never heard of, and had difficulty finding on our Admiralty charts for Cornerbrook, then Dingwall Nova Scotia for gypsum to Brooklyn, New York. By 1945 Dingwall was populated entirely by Scots who had never given up any of their national traditions. They wore kilts, held ceilidhs, ate haggis, played the bagpipes and wondered why they had ever come to live in such a godforsaken part of the world. There seemed little change when I passed through again several years later.

It took just two days to discharge the full cargo of gypsum at Brooklyn, and we had one night ashore in Manhattan. By then I knew and liked New York better than any city in the UK other than my hometown of Glasgow, but I wouldn't have wanted to live there. A young singer called Frank Sinatra was doing quite well on Broadway, but a young female singer well known to everyone in Britain was doing even better. When I asked one of the stevedores where he was likely to be going that evening he said, 'I stay home, this is the night Gracie Fields is on the radio'. Coming from a hard-bitten docker from Brooklyn, that was quite a tribute.

More crew members were logged on this trip for desertion, absence without leave, and refusal to work than on any other trip I have taken before or since. The short period in New York accounted for some of them, but it was Cornerbrook in Newfoundland, where we discharged pulp wood for Bowaters, that we lost most of them. Girls from all over the province descended on the place daily, hoping for work in the paper mills. Most of the local men were serving overseas and the girls waited anxiously outside the dock gates and in the nearest cafes for seamen to come ashore. At sailing time I went round in a taxi picking them up and returning them to the ship where Blackwood was waiting on the bridge with his log book handy. As soon as I got them on board they were logged and fined. He chose me to rope them in and said, 'You go and collect them, Second Mate – you'll know where to find them.' I didn't like the way he said that.

The ship then sailed to Newport News, Virginia to load coal for St. Johns for bunkering ships on arrival or before they left; this took twelve days before we went up to another outpost for a cargo of pit props for the UK and returned to St. Johns in time to celebrate VJ Day on the 15th of August 1945. The World War was over, and we sailed all the way across the North Atlantic on our own for the first time since I had gone to sea in 1941. It was a very strange feeling. I signed off the *Douglas* in Hull, went home and got married on the 12th of September. We had said that, after all, we'd wait until war ended.

After seven days' honeymoon in the Ailsa Hotel at Girvan in Ayrshire, it was time to get another ship. I wanted a change from the Baron Line and went to the Merchant Navy Officer's Pool on James Watt Street in Glasgow. They sent me over to Govan Docks with a view to joining the *Bradford City* as Second Mate; the ship was owned by another tramp ship company, Reardon Smith of Cardiff. She was a fairly new motor vessel and quite different to the old ships I had previously sailed on. It was a change of company but not quite such a change in working conditions. I didn't know at the time that Reardon Smith's shipowning knowledge had been acquired from his long association with 'Hungry Hogarth'. The ship was diesel-propelled and very different in that respect from the old coalburners I was used to. Smiths was one of the first British shipping companies to operate motor vessels. Harry, the Chief Engineer, had the first ever diesel endorsement to be stamped on a steam certificate. The Board of Trade examiner didn't have one himself but had a book describing a marine diesel engine. The examination consisted of one question and one answer. 'Tell me what you know about motor ships.' Harry told him and he said, 'That sounds all right, you've passed.'

As far as I was concerned, my training in the Baron Line was just right for the new company. The master was from north Wales and

Baron Herries.

knew how to run a tight ship. One of the jobs on my first Saturday was to issue the men's subs. The money totalled £30. Captain W. C. Thomas gave me £29 10s. and said the Third Mate owed him 10s and if I could get it from him I would have my £30. He wasn't a man to argue with. I issued the money as instructed and told the galley boy to wait until last, then sent him round to see the Third Mate for his 10s. He was so surprised that he paid him on the spot.

We had another week in Glasgow discharging cargo and getting rid of another white elephant that we had inherited from the war – long steel derricks with nets which dropped down over both sides of the ship as a protection against torpedoes. There was no proof that they ever worked.

We had no trouble signing on real seamen for the trip across to the States to load a cargo of grain at Portland, Maine for London. They were all men from the highlands and islands, brought up in boats, and they had been at sea all their lives. We signed on a bosun first and let him choose the others. They were all well known to each other and in some cases were related. After some of the white crews I had sailed with on previous ships, it was quite a revelation. Sailing in ballast, and irrespective of the North Atlantic weather, the cargo holds were prepared to start loading on arrival: heavy seamanlike work which with most other crews would have been delayed until the ship docked.

Unfortunately crew nepotism also had a downside. When one packed in they all did, and after a difference of opinion when the ship arrived in London on Christmas Eve, all of them were paid off and went home.

Captain Thomas told me to get a train to Glasgow, have Christmas Day there and travel back on Boxing Day ready to start work the following morning 'and bring the wife back with you'. The Baron Line didn't allow that, but Smiths encouraged it.

Rationing at home didn't improve for a number of years after the war ended. We each brought a turkey and a chicken back from Portland; the turkeys weighed between 25 and 30 pounds. The ship's chandler had nothing smaller. I thought cooking one would be difficult. In true American style the foreman stevedore said it was no problem, he had cooked a 35-pounder at home the previous year. I asked how he managed it. 'Well, it's like this,' he said. 'Its ass was in the oven and its neck was out de front door.' The weather was cold out on deck and the First Mate and I were warming him up with a bottle of Scotch trying to get him to load the ship on a more even keel. The manner they were pouring in the grain, it was uphill or downhill all the way along the deck.

As I took the wrong train at Euston my short time at home was even shorter. I had to sleep overnight on a settee in the main lounge of the Station Hotel at Preston and the next train to Glasgow was 1.00 p.m. on Christmas Day. The cleaners told me to stay on the settee until breakfast time and they would move it around as necessary; it was very accommodating of them, and I needed the rest.

My luggage consisted of a large cardboard suitcase containing the turkey and chicken and a small canvas bag with a couple of shirts and a bottle of Scotch. In order to keep an eye on my very valuable cargo, I stowed it on the luggage rack opposite and the only other passenger, also a Preston/Glasgow casualty from the previous night, sat underneath.

Travelling on trains in wartime and long after that was a very cold and uncomfortable experience, particularly during the winter, so it was rather surprising to see my travelling companion wiping sweat off his head with a handkerchief. The turkey was thawing out! I opened the bottle of whisky and that kept us both happy until we arrived at the Central Station. It was rather a flying visit and we arrived back on board the ship in London the following evening. The ship loaded a full general cargo for South Africa which included a consignment of the first new cars built in the UK since before the War. They were Hillman Minxes, with radios, which the London dockers found too difficult to resist pilfering, along with many other choice items from the cargo. This led to much police activity aboard the ship and ashore, with house searches and criminal proceedings which delayed our sailing. Because of that my wife had a wonderful time. She was up in London every day. A lot of the City was missing but the aura, the Cockney spirit and hospitality, were still there.

We called at Capetown, Durban and Port Elizabeth to discharge the cargo, and then we went on to Lorenzo Marques to load coal for South America.

From Lorenzo Marques we made a fairly long passage round the Cape and across the South Atlantic to Buenos Aires. I was getting quite used to sailing all over the place without any worries about 'outside interference'. Although the war was over, merchant ships were still under the control of the Ministry of War Transport and sailed according to its instructions. East Africa to Buenos Aires with coal and from there to the UK with grain may seem to have been a long haul for cargoes like that, but the urgent necessity for solid fuel in the Argentine and for food in Britain was still there then and would be for some time to come.

We spent almost two weeks in Buenos Aires and had more time ashore than we'd had four years previously on the *Renfrew*. The senior wireless operator on that ship had joined the *Bradford City* in London and we decided to investigate further some of the more interesting places we had been to. Very little had changed. Two successive Saturdays were spent at the races, one of the Argentine's favourite sports. At Palermo in Buenos Aires we pooled our money, bet on every race and lost the lot. The following week we caught the 'racing train' down to La Plata, pooled our money and had a winner in every race but one. The ship was sailing the following day and the pesos had to be spent. We started at the racecourse by ordering gold-top bottles of beer instead of ordinary ones. Then we headed back to Buenos Aires where we ate the largest steaks I'd ever seen while trying to work out what to do with all the other pesos. I bought a leather suitcase and filled it up with everything that was unlikely to be subject to customs duty. We discharged the grain in Belfast and I decided to sign off the ship, get the ferry over to Glasgow and have some home leave. Reardon Smith were very considerate and told me to get in touch with the office when I wished to go back to sea. At that time there were no company contracts for officers like me who were employed trip by trip. A couple of weeks later I joined the *Indian City* at Tyne Dock; as soon as I went on board the shore super handed me an envelope with full pay for the time at home.

I made several trips on *Indian City*, one of which was up the Freetown River in West Africa for ore to the Tyne, one to Cuba for a cargo of sugar and another to Haifa in Palestine where we loaded 80,000 cases of Jaffa oranges.

The voyage to Cuba started from the Tyne and continued around the North of Scotland and from there by Great Circle down to Santa Cruz Del Sur for sugar. The Captain was a senior man from Bideford, where all the ships were registered, and the First Mate was from Cardiff. I was Second Mate and the Captain's son, who was serving his time as an apprentice, had just been promoted to uncertificated Third Mate.

The first surprise came just before sailing when the Old Man asked if I had a sextant. Until then I had thought all deck officers on foreign-going ships had sextants until I discovered that I was the only one on *Indian City*. Mine was 1914 vintage and had navigated a lifeboat into Capetown during the First World War. It cost £6 through an advert in the Tech when I was there studying for Second Mate and so far it had served me well, though always with some backup by the master and other deck officers. That clearly couldn't happen in this case as my old sextant wasn't easy to adjust, and so was difficult to use with any accuracy. It was a 'one man job', so all navigation at sea would be my responsibility.

On the 11th of August we passed through the Pentland Firth and I set the courses down towards the Windward Passage between Haiti and Cuba. Each day at noon the Old Man would come up to the chartroom and say, 'Where are we now, Second Mate?' On the 24th he asked, 'When are we going to pick up land?' I said noon the next day and prayed it would happen; it didn't; there was a heat haze with restricted visibility, and the Old Man was beginning to mutter under his breath something about 'this is the way we lose miles'; I was worried until a bit of very low-lying land showed up abeam. Isla San Salvador was in the right place after all.

The other trips on *Indian City* were similar to the first one. The sugar was discharged in Liverpool and the large leather suitcase was very useful. We filled it with sugar and put it on the quay beside the

Indian City.

ship where my wife waited for a taxi to the railway station. As the ship was leaving the quay I could see the driver struggling to lift the heavy suitcase into his cab. Sugar was still severely rationed and still scarce in 1946, so it was a load of very valuable contraband she smuggled through the dock gate. Like most policemen, Scousers were always very courteous to ladies.

Captain Harris was different in many ways to any other Master with whom I sailed. He didn't like change, and for that reason didn't trust the Brown's Gyro Compass which Smiths had just started putting on board their ships. I would tell the helmsman to steer the true course by gyro, and when I left the wheelhouse he would tell him to use the old magnetic compass instead. He never objected when he saw it had been altered back to gyro; I think he was just making a point, or points, as it was a recurring process.

The ship loaded ore in Pepel for the Tyne. I threw an old pair of trousers down to a bumboat and up came a monkey. In addition to women, monkeys were banned on board Baron boats, but not on Reardon Smith's ships, at least not by Captain Harris, whose one proviso when I was exercising the monkey on the lower bridge was, 'Don't let the b..... thing into my cabin, he'll p... and s... all over the place.' It was in my cabin most of the time until we reached the Tyne and it did nothing like that. As my wife was coming down to the ship for a few days I told the apprentices to look after the monkey until we sailed. When my wife had gone home I asked for the monkey and was told they sold it for £15 and had spent the money ashore. What else could I have expected from apprentices? It was all part of the job. That particular monkey turned out to be a very rare species.

My next trip on that ship was to Haifa to load a full cargo of oranges for London. Although it was December, the weather in the eastern Mediterranean was very warm and the orange boxes were in the holds for more than three weeks before they started unloading. The London dockers got wind of them and, understandably on this occasion, refused to discharge thousands of boxes stowed at the bottom of the holds. There were hundreds of gallons of 'fresh' orange juice swilling around and it was unlikely that the shippers, whoever they were, would think of carrying oranges in that way again. The cargo holds on tramp ships were made of steel and were suitable for the carriage of coal, iron ore, grain, bags of sugar and other cargoes, but not for fresh fruit. The ship was still sailing under the Ministry, who were not unused to losing ships and all their contents, so three quarters of a cargo of Jaffas wasn't too bad considering the scarcities which existed ashore.

It was more than five years since I'd been to Haifa. It was still a nice port of call, but by the time the ship passed Malta on her way home on Christmas Day, the previous attraction of drinking fresh orange juice had evaporated. The smell of rotting oranges coming up through the cargo-hold ventilators had started to seep into every corner of the ship. It would be a long time after that cargo was discharged before I would enjoy eating another orange.

The most excited member of the crew was Sparks. Our Radio Officer was a Jew from Manchester, and ever since he had been a small boy he had looked forward to visiting the 'land of his fathers'. He was a very good shipmate and I looked forward to showing him around Haifa as soon as we got there. It was disappointing and I was very sorry for him, as he was no more welcome there than anyone else.

I sailed on *Indian City* until the time came for me to go ashore to study for my First Mate's certificate. However, after just a few days, I felt it would be better to get a bit more money to keep me in the manner to which I had then become accustomed. Studying for my certificate meant two months at the Tech without any earnings, so I decided to go back to sea, if only for a short time.

CHAPTER 3

Olynthus & Hong Siang

When I first saw *Olynthus*, the old steam oil tanker was anchored at Seleter Naval Base off Singapore Island. The ship wasn't much to look at, but it was good to get the job as Second Mate to deliver her to a UK port.

I had decided to go back home after a short period as a deck officer on a Hong Kong registered ship carrying passengers and freight between Burma, Malaya and the China Coast. This was an opportunity to work my passage there and get paid for it. The plans to leave Glasgow for a new life in the Far East were cut short when I received a telegram from my wife letting me know that a baby was underway.

The Straits Steamship Company rightly felt their responsibilities ended when I stepped ashore from their *Hong Siang* on arrival back in Singapore in May 1947. My term of engagement was for five years

Hong Siang.

but the Company was aware of the difficulty involved in getting back home without their support. I hadn't given that much thought until I left the ship with little money and no prospects.

Up until then I had sailed on six different foreign-going cargo ships, but none like *Hong Siang*. She was a completely new and unique experience. There was a British master and deck officers, Indian and Chinese engineers, and 125 Chinese deck and engine crew. Passengers numbered between 1200 and 1500 souls. At that time there was no other way than by ship to transport large numbers of people from Malaya to Hong Kong and Communist China. Down below in the cargo holds the steel 'tweendecks were marked out in sections for families to share. Fathers, mothers, the old and the young, as well as countless children, all squeezed together in their restricted bit of steel deck space and lay on whatever they had brought with them for the purpose. The average distance travelled by the human cargo down in the holds of the ship was about 2000 miles. Passengers usually on board for at least a week.

On this vessel all passengers and cargo were handled by senior Chinese crew members who had been specially appointed by the Company. Our job on the bridge was to get the ship from one port to another quickly and safely. It wasn't quite as easy as it sounds. Most lighthouses and other navigational aids had been deliberately destroyed by the Japanese and sailing at night between so many islands and through narrow channels and passages was very challenging. There was no radar, only magnetic compasses and seamen's intuitions. The Company had three ships doing similar work on the China Coast. One, the *Hong Mo*, had already sunk with hundreds of deck passengers on board, and the loss of life had never in fact been accurately estimated. Some time later the *Hong Keng* suffered the same fate. I never heard what eventually happened to *Hong Siang*.

The Master of this ship was unfortunately completely 'unapproachable'. The First Mate had served in the RNR during the war. The other Second Mate had been an apprentice with a notorious Cardiff tramp ship company. He had just begun serving his time at the start of the war when his ship was torpedoed; he was taken prisoner and spent most of the next five years a POW in Germany. When he was released the company wouldn't employ him again as he was considered too old to take up where he had left off and, because of lack of experience, he was no good to them. He persevered, got a sympathetic hearing elsewhere, and had just passed the exam for Second Mate before joining this vessel.

The ship's officers and first-class passengers had nice cabins upon the boat deck. During the times the vessel was at sea, that area was completely segregated for protection purposes by locked gates, spiked bulwarks and other obstructions to deter piracy, always a threat in those waters when carrying large numbers of Chinese deck passengers. A substantial armoury on the bridge of the ship was ready for use at all times.

By early March 1947 the uncertainties of war were being replaced by the uncertainties of peace. It was time to take stock, and, like countless others, I had to consider the future carefully. Despite the loss of more than 11,000,000 gross tons of British Merchant Shipping between 1939 and 1945, there were more opportunities at sea at the end of the war than when it had started. Ship losses had been more than amply replaced by frantic new building programmes in Canada, the USA and the UK. The 35,000 British and Commonwealth seamen who went down with the ships couldn't be replaced then, and never have been.

I had enjoyed tramping around the world in cargo ships during and after the war, but nevertheless wanted a change. There were plenty of openings for certificated officers on every class of vessel. The job with Straits SS Company based in Singapore advertised in *The Glasgow Herald* looked too good to refuse. Within days I was boarding the troopship *Otranto* at Tilbury, bound for Malaya via Suez. This vessel had a remarkable record of service, having carried thousands of troops and other forces personnel from and to all the various battlegrounds. On this occasion, even with the War over, she was fully 'booked' with troops and a large number of cabin passengers like myself. Some were going out East to work there for

Otranto.

the first time; many others had done it all before and were returning to the UK, having been imprisoned by the Japanese when they invaded Burma, the Malay States, Singapore, Borneo and Sarawak. Separate two-berth first-class cabins on *Otranto* were knocked into large dormitories containing ten or twelve bunks. I had never travelled anywhere before in first-class accommodation, albeit in the rather close company of others.

Before we sailed from Tilbury I went into Lloyds Bank to change three Scottish five pound notes for English money. Scottish notes such as fivers weren't always acceptable currency, and in many places in the UK there was commission to pay for their exchange or use. *Otranto* was an English-registered ship and I didn't want to take the chance. The teller in the bank studied the notes carefully and said to take them along Fenchurch Street to their foreign exchange department. I decided then and there that if I ever had a bank account it wouldn't be with Lloyds.

The passage to Singapore took twenty-three days. Apart from officers, all the troops were segregated from the passengers. There was no alcholic drink sold on board, which didn't go down well with some of my travelling companions. In the bar it was lemonade, coca cola and bingo. We drank one another's health with a rationed amount of ginger beer and looked forward to getting ashore at Port Said. We agreed to smuggle one bottle of liquor each back aboard the ship. It worked well and even before *Otranto* entered the Suez Canal broaching had started. My £15 had swelled considerably, as I had won a sweepstake by estimating accurately a ship's day's run. During those twenty-four hours, one of the courses was between Cape Bon in Tunisia and the island of Pantelleria. Having been through there just two months earlier as navigating officer on my last ship it wasn't too difficult to determine the effect the tidal stream and current would have on *Otranto*'s speed in the area. I had been surprised when we had sailed there in January how much influence it had had on *Indian City*.

With one exception, my travelling companions had spent several years as prisoners of war of the Japanese in Malaya, Borneo and Sarawak. We took turns each evening before dinner to provide aperitifs all round. As fare-paying passengers we were allowed ashore again at Aden and topped up supplies for the long haul to Singapore.

Day and night the public address system belted out dos and don'ts and other commands to the troops. Unfortunately the alleyways were festooned with loudspeakers and some passengers took the liberty to disconnect them where necessary. The colonel in charge of the troops promised that anyone found doing that would be put ashore at the next port. This happened to be Aden, one of the most godforsaken places in the world. The loudspeaker problem was solved. OC (Officer Commanding) Troops apparently seemed to have more authority over passengers than did the master of the ship. There were no exemptions from the punishment, fare-paying or not.

There were many first-hand accounts of Japanese atrocities after Singapore fell. Each person had his own personal story of the way he was treated, some much worse than others. They all had had one thing in common, a belief that Singapore Island was impregnable. Some joined the Local Defence Volunteers but didn't have the chance to do any defending. As they put it, 'The Japs came in through the back door before we knew they were anywhere near.' The Japanese decreed that, 'Having worn a uniform it qualified men to work on the Railway' – the Railway being the dreaded Burma/Siam Railroad where many thousands of British and Colonial servicemen died, in horrific conditions, from the barbaric treatment they were subjected to by the captors. One of our fellow passengers suffered the experience and survived. His brother, who also joined the Volunteers, did not – he died on the Railway right alongside him.

Perhaps the stories we listened to at that time didn't have the impact they have on us now, more than fifty years later. What we knew about it seemed at the time to have a less horrifying effect than it does now. Perhaps six years of bitter war which most of us had experienced one way or another hadn't left much room for surprises. There were many on board *Otranto* going out East to try to start again. There were also those going out for the first time to join husbands and others already there. One of our cabin group had opened an exporting business in the UK. He was advised to get to

Singapore as soon as possible, 'before the Eastern Gold Rush commences'. He did just that and booked into the Adelphi Hotel for an indefinite stay.

When *Otranto* arrived, many of her passengers didn't know what to expect after disembarking. Singapore was, and still is, one of the most intriguing ports in the world. Not all the Japanese POWs had been repatriated. They shuffled around during the night, sweeping the very streets that their armies had marched along so triumphantly. Their heads were kept down and they never spoke, even to one another. Their disgrace was absolute.

The company sent me to one of their vessels in drydock while I was awaiting the arrival of my own ship. Using the 'Darvel' on a full board basis without having to work offered wonderful opportunities to discover Singapore. I took them with great enthusiasm but also discovered that the 90+ fahrenheit temperatures every day were unsuitable for walking around a golf course. I also discovered that in the early 1940s the Japanese hadn't played golf. They had dug up the courses to grow food.

I eventually joined *Hong Siang*, which was anchored off the port, loading cargo from lighters. There was a swarm of men around the decks, a few were working, many others weren't. When the cargo was dealt with, and everything was battened down, it was time to embark the passengers. They clambered up the accommodation ladder by the dozen, carrying their children and their sparse belongings. They were checked on board, then herded down the cargo holds, vying with each other for the best bit of deck space. The ship tried to leave once the first-class passengers had embarked. Even with the engine going full ahead she wouldn't move. Someone had forgotten that the ship's draft should never exceed the depth of water. The Old Man just said, 'Second Mate, I think we're stuck, ring off the engines and we'll have another go later; check the draught, take some soundings, then stay on the bridge until she floats, and let me know.' In the circumstances it seemed a casual reaction.

From the bridge I saw some movement of the canvas cover on the starboard forward lifeboat. I instructed the quartermaster to uncover the boat. Crouched down inside were several Chinese stowaways. I told him to get the crew to uncover the other lifeboats. They were all similarly occupied. I was later informed that the sailors' perks were a choice of the stowaways' belongings. The sailors smuggled stowaways into the lifeboats, took from them whatever they could, and at convenient times after the ship sailed they were dispersed down the holds among hundreds of others already there. Sailing the China Seas was different from sailing anywhere else. Human values were different there, and life was cheap.

On the second night at sea the quartermaster reported to the bridge that there had been two deaths and one birth. I asked him to send the Indian doctor up with a report. The doctor duly arrived, walking with a 'Western Ocean Roll' (although the sea was calm), a flushed complexion, and looking rather surprised at being summoned for such an unimportant event.

My suggestion was to call the Captain in case he might wish to bury the bodies at sea. He said, 'We don't bother the Captain with things like that, besides, burial has already taken place.' The doctor left the bridge to resume whatever pastime he had been indulging in when we had interrupted him. I made an entry of the incident in the bridge log book, signed it, and never heard it mentioned again.

There were no POWs working in the streets of Hong Kong. The port seemed to have made a full recovery from the oppression and hardships suffered under occupation. Once again the ship anchored well off, and the juggling of cargo and human beings started rightaway. Traditionally, the former owners, who were now the ships' agents, entertained the captain and two or three officers to dinner in Hong Kong's top hotel. I was one of the chosen three but what looked to be an interesting and enjoyable evening was very much marred when a cabin boy found the Mate collapsed in the shower. He was taken to hospital in Hong Kong. The trip ashore went ahead. There were five men and five Chinese girls arranged by the hosts alternately around the table. They could all speak English and the girl on the right was the companion for the evening. It was a first ever opportunity to meet socially and converse with real Chinese. There was plenty of time to talk, with a bit of dancing between courses. There were lots of different courses; and the eating, dancing and talking went on for several hours. I hoped to learn something about Hong Kong and China but found out that my Chinese companion had just arrived there herself. She had come ashore that day from a Ben Line ship from San Francisco to do social work in China. The idea was that a young, much travelled British ship's officer could in some way enlighten her. She was a very good dancer and we parted very satisfied with the food, the company, and the ship agent's hospitality, but with both of us still wondering about China and the real Chinese.

The following day, just before the ship was ready to sail, we were informed that the Mate had died in hospital from a cerebral haemorrhage. The Port Authority wanted to detain the ship until another Mate with a Master's Certificate was signed on. The Captain's protests that it was impossible to get anyone at short notice, if at all, and that he would do the Mate's watch himself, was only agreed because the next passages, to Swatow and Amoy and back to Hong Kong, would only take a few days. The ship wouldn't be allowed to leave then for Singapore until a fully certificated First Mate was found.

For a change we tied alongside jetties in Swatow and Amoy. Before the ship was anywhere near its berth men were clambering up the mooring ropes. The sailors knew what to do. They allowed the ropes to slacken off, then quickly heaved away, catapulting the men into the water. I never knew if any of the stowaways made it to the deck or how many free passages there were. The squalid living and working conditions in these places were appalling. In 1947, this was the real Chinese. I wondered then how an American-born Chinese girl from San Francisco could possibly succeed with social work in that country. It was clear then that the rapid growth of Communism was inevitable.

We arrived back to anchor off Hong Kong and stayed there for several days. It was a very different place, with different people, British and Chinese working hard together to re-develop its great potential as a major Far East city and seaport. For the time being, criticism of the way in which the Japanese had just walked in and taken control was forgotten. It was said that there would never be any Communism in Hong Kong and Kowloon. In 1947, and for many years after that, this seemed quite convincing.

The ship spent several days anchored off Hong Kong. With our limited cargo duties in port, there was plenty of time to get to know the place, and, of course, neighbouring Kowloon. There were sufficient attractions for sailors ashore in both places, but traditionally the first night there on the return passage was devoted to on-board entertainment in one of the larger cabins on the bridge deck. On that occasion it was the turn of one of the engineers to provide both the entertainment and the drinks. This was the officers' first social get-together since the ship had sailed from Singapore. The cabin became really cramped in a short space of time when a number of Chinese girls squeezed themselves in. A sampan full of them had come alongside and they had distributed themselves throughout the vessel. They seemed to know their way around. A couple of hours later, when I got back to my cabin and switched on the light, two of them were sitting there in the dark, expectantly. When they were told to go they just smiled, then giggled to one another and padded off along the deck in the direction of the sampan for the return trip to Hong Kong. They would have been in good time for less disappointing encounters ashore in Wanchai.

It was easy to understand why sailing the China Coast was popular with most seamen, particularly on a ship such as *Hong Siang*. I had only worked on tramp ships since going to sea, and so the food, accommodation and personal attention that a deck officer received on that vessel was unimaginable. That was a life it was easy to get used to and probably difficult to get away from. Coming off watch during the day, I would find a set of 'whites' washed, ironed and laid out on the bunk with a large cold bottle of Tennants Ale standing on the cabin table. Dinner in the evening was à la carte. Everything and anything you asked for would be available wothout exception.

My cabin on *Hong Siang* was on the starboard side of the bridgedeck; the other Second Mate's cabin – his name was Gerry, in this case – was on the port side. The morning after the officers' get-together, the steward brought a silver tray with two full breakfasts up to Gerry's room. The captain was having his morning stroll around the accommodation and from one side to another across the bridge deck. Gerry and one of the girls, suitably undressed, were in the bunk with the window wide open. Later I said to him, 'The old man must have seen you having breakfast in bed with that nude sampan girl.' He said, 'She's not a sampan girl, she's a nice young lady. Anyway he does it himself.' I asked him, 'What about VD? It's rife up here, and you're taking a chance.' 'There is no chance as far as I am concerned; when it used to happen I had to pay for treatment, but not now. I have my own supply and can inject myself when necessary. During the years as a POW in Germany you learn to live with some deprivations but you also learn what to do about others.'

All the cargo work was carried out at anchor and there were sampans available at all times for transport ashore. I got to know Hong Kong and Kowloon quite well by both day and night. Although it was just a short time since the Japanese had been ousted, the port and city of Hong Kong were developing and thriving as if nothing unusual had ever happened.

The new Mate joined the ship the day before we sailed for Singapore. He looked quite old, all of 45 years of age. The Captain called him a China Coast dropout and said his only interest in the man was the Master's certificate, as without that we wouldn't be allowed to sail. And, during the entire trip from Hong Kong to Singapore, the old man didn't allow the new Mate on the bridge. He and the Indian doctor socialised together down in their cabins with as many bottles of 'John Barleycorn' as they required. The Mate was the first off in Singapore and thanked us for a very nice trip.

On the beach with no job, a few dollars in my pocket, and thousands of miles from the UK should have been a daunting situation. At the time it wasn't of any concern, just another exciting experience. There was no immediate prospect of getting back home, and unlike the hospitality I had received in other ports from such as the 'Sally Ann' and Missions to Seamen, board and lodgings had to be paid for. After a few days spent calling without success at ship agents' offices, and not wanting to get back to the UK as a penniless DBS (Distressed British Seaman), I contacted my former *Otranto* cabin Mate, who by then had his export business well underway. Like many other British companies, he represented Mercer's Chronometers but hadn't yet had time to sell them in Singapore. As a seaman I was the ideal person to get that agency off the ground; besides, every ship in the world had a Mercer's chronometer. Somehow that message hadn't reached the Chinese and Malay ship people in Singapore. Despite exploring every back street which was reputed to secrete owners' and agents' offices, I didn't sell a single clock. I was always courteously received, offered a drink and sometimes a job, but that was it. My friend did his best to encourage me by paying quite liberal expenses and saying, 'The first call is the worst; when you go back another time and they know you, business will roll in.' Although I worked for about a week there was still no sign of any business so there were no second calls.

Living in the hostel at the time was a former First Mate of a British ship who had come ashore from an oil tanker with no intention of going back, and had set himself up there on a kind of permanent basis working for local interests operating small coastal ships from Singapore to the outlying islands. He offered me a job shifting large landing craft from Keppel Island to berths in the port. The work couldn't have been better. I was taken over by small boat to the island before dawn and assisted by two Malay seamen who looked after the engines and handled the mooring ropes, I steered the craft round to Singapore Harbour and tied up there alongside a quay wall. It wasn't exactly a masterpiece of navigation and the money was quite out of proportion to the work and time involved.

The jerry cans, along with whatever else was stowed beneath them in the landing craft, were off-loaded into coasters. At the time I didn't care what it was or where it was going. Large quantities of military equipment had been cleared from the mainland for storage on Keppel Island at the end of the War. Singapore was a Free Port and there were large movements of all kinds of vessels without too much interference from ashore. It was a good set-up for many types of doubtful trading.

After a number of successful moves I was offered a job to take one of the small ships to Java/Sumatra. During the time this was being discussed I read a newspaper advert for deck officers to deliver a ship from Singapore to the UK. I went to see the agents and was engaged as Second Mate on an oil tanker. It was just a run job so my lack of tanker experience didn't matter.

A first consideration was to get home as soon as possible and I turned down the chance of a very early promotion to master, albeit on a small vessel. I arrived back in the UK four months later and read that a British ship's officer who had tried to get to Java/Sumatra with a cargo of ammunition and military stores had been stopped by the Dutch and sentenced to fifteen years in prison. The blockade of Indonesia by Dutch patrol vessels hadn't been mentioned when I was working in Singapore; it became clear why the trip money offered by my hostel friend to take a ship over there was so very generous.

The instructions the First Mate and I were given from the *Olynthus*' agents were to go immediately to the naval base, take over the ship from the RFA and get her round to Singapore. We could have a tug in case the engines weren't working, and the pilot would know where the anchorage was to be. There was sufficient crew on board and much to be done to her before sailing for the UK. This really was a new experience. Both of us had signed many receipts for stores and equipment but never a receipt for a whole ship.

Olynthus had been a fleet oiler during the war and seemed to have done nothing else since. We were greeted very warmly by the RFA captain, who seemed to be the only deck officer on board. Considering the long period the vessel had been laid up and the condition she appeared to be in, we wondered what the large number of Chinese and Malay crew members had done to pass the time away. The Captain's beautiful stewardess would have had plenty to do looking after him. When we were there she was hanging the washing on a clothes line on the lower bridge. I asked if she was a member of the crew as we were signing most of them on new articles. He said she wasn't qualified to work on a ship and could only be signed on as a supernumerary. Fortunately there would be no vacancies available in that capacity.

The Mate was on the bridge with the pilot; I was on the forecastle head. Luckily the port anchor had not been used to moor the ship, as when the starboard one came clear of the water, it was so heavily covered with marine growth that it looked like a huge toffee apple dangling from the hawsepipe. It was going to be impossible to use it until it was cleaned off in drydock, whenever that was to be.

The anchorage we were allocated was so far off the port of Singapore that it involved a small voyage in a good-sized boat to get there. The ship had no form of transport on board, not even a lifeboat of any description. Suitably certified boats were being shipped from the UK, but no one knew when they were due to arrive in Singapore.

After anchoring, our cursory inspection around the decks of *Olynthus* was less encouraging than we had hoped. There were large amounts of expensive and unused equipment on board, some of which was beginning to rot away, such as the mooring ropes, for example. There were also many lengths of oiling-at-sea hoses and other gear used for those purposes. In addition to the lifeboats, there were many essential items missing without which the vessel couldn't sail. As navigating officer, my priority was to get hold of corrected and updated Admiralty charts. I felt at that particular time that this was too much to hope for. I was right, and many days were spent correcting the charts that were available and, where necessary, constructing large-scale plans from small-scale charts with the help of some recent copies of Admiralty Sailing Directions for the most difficult areas.

Three weeks later, the Captain and Chief Engineer employed by the London ship deliverers arrived on board. It wasn't a moment too soon, as the Mate had been hard at it flogging as much of the 'surplus' ship's gear as he could. It was standard practice on many ships for the Mate to sell old mooring ropes when they were considered unsuitable for further use, but usually with the Captain's co-operation. This one wanted to flog as much as he could before the Captain even joined the ship. As he was my senior officer and in charge of the vessel at the time, there was little I could do about it, apart from making a few contentious comments. When I did, he reminded me the ship had been accepted as it lay, there was no inventory of contents and apart from us nobody knew what was on board. I didn't like this at all and thought that he was in the wrong, but his assumption was to prove correct. Very considerately he suggested I turn in one afternoon for a couple of hours. My Cabin was on the starboard after end of the midship accommodation. I heard rasping noises, looked out and saw the valuable metal-bound oiling hoses being loaded through a fairlead into a sampan.

Captain Alan Baxter was a good seaman and a very good shipmate. Fortunately he was also an experienced tanker man, having served his apprenticeship with Shell. He informed us right away that the ship would load in the Persian Gulf en route to the UK. By this time we realised how much work and effort was required to make her seaworthy, if indeed this was possible. The only time I had spent ashore since anchoring was to check the two lifeboats when they

The tug, *Bustler.*

arrived on a Blue Funnel ship. The only way ashore was by shipchandler's boat and took almost a full day there and back. I had been told that the standard on Blue Funnel vessels was the highest in the country, if not the world. This was one of their US-acquired wartime models and our two lifeboats were stowed on top of one of the forward hatches. I examined the condition of the boats and signed for them under protest. They had been loaded in Liverpool and been on board for several weeks in all kinds of weather. They had been carried uncovered in the most exposed part of the ship, and when he was asked, the Third Mate admitted that they had put no water in the bottom of the boats to help prevent the timbers from opening out in extremely hot conditions. If that visit did nothing else, it dispelled any inferior feelings there might have been about sailing with the Baron Line and Reardon Smith. None of the ships I had been on would have carried valuable cargo such as other ships' lifeboats in that way.

Baxter's last job before joining us in Singapore was to deliver the battleship *Warspite* to Metal Industries in Scotland. Everyone knows, of course, that they never made it there. The ship went ashore in bad weather in Mounts Bay, Cornwall, and became a total loss.

At the round-table meeting before the big event, discussion had hinged upon the number of tugs needed for the passage. *Bustler*, allegedly the largest and best tug in the world, was proposed by Metal Industries as being the only one necessary. As he would be in charge of the tow, Alan Baxter insisted on a second tug in case the weather turned bad. They refused and put their own superintendent on the tug. Baxter and his men went on *Warspite*. The rest is history

The decision by Metal Industries to just have one tug for the tow was clearly financial, but for their ships' superintendent to agree to such an un-seamanlike arrangement could have been professional suicide. When an experienced man like Alan Baxter said a second tug was a necessity and they disagreed there could be no compromise.

The weather turned foul, Bustler's towing spring parted and the ship started to drift towards the shore. They got the end of another line on board the battleship, and as Baxter and his men were about to heave it in on the windlass the superintendent on the bridge of the tug, fearing that they were getting too close to the ship's bow, went ahead on his engines and pulled the rope off. The ship drifted towards the beach and went aground. In that kind of weather two tugs were required. I wondered what the underwriters said about it and whether any insurance claims were approved.

A Scottish radio officer, a Second Engineer and a Third Mate joined *Olynthus*. Like myself, they had all been 'on the beach' and were looking for a run job back home.

Sparks was a China Coast man and before the war he had lived in various apartments in Shanghai with 'home helps'; he said it had been a good way to go to sea when he felt like it. With the post-war situation as it was, there was no way he could go back; he tried his luck in Singapore, but it wasn't the same any more, and after less than a year he was heading back to Glasgow. He said the Straits Chinese were different, the lifestyle in Shanghai was cheaper and better. It was too hot in Singapore and it rained every day. He was a rotund, pleasant chap and, as wireless operators on ships in peacetime didn't really do any work when a ship is in port, and not too much when at sea, he was a good Mate for going ashore with Baxter on his periodic trips to the agents. The old man told me not to order too many stores at any one time and to make sure the deliveries were as frequent as possible. This ensured at least one daily boat service from the chandler and a 'gratuitous' return to the ship as required.

I accompanied them on a sortie ashore. Baxter insisted I get off the ship for a break and leave the other Mates to get on with it. The chandler's hospitality got the day off to a flying start. Sparks and the Old Man were seasoned campaigners and the whiskies didn't appear to have too much effect. We went on to several places traditionally frequented by sailors, including a couple of very memorable places. Everything was available in 'The Great World' and 'Happy World', from table tennis to close-contact dances with lovely hostesses. I was awakened early the following afternoon feeling I had made it to the Next World. Looking down at me on the bed was a very wrinkled, sombre-looking Malay woman's face, which broke into a smile of relief as I opened my eyes. At some point during the previous night's perambulations, I must have run out of steam, and in order to carry on without me, the others had checked me into a hotel, paid the room in advance and thoughtfully pinned a note on my shirt with the address and telephone number of the shipchandler's office.

I got back to the ship several hours later to find Sparks and Alan Baxter sitting in the cabin with a bottle of Scotch on the table. The offer to have 'a hair of the dog that bit me' was politely refused. They both looked in perfect condition, and I headed for my bunk. It had been an unforgettable night out, but not an experience that I wanted to repeat in a hurry.

Our Second Engineer had spent the war as a POW of the Japanese, locked up in Changi Jail. He had joined the Singapore Fire Service a few days before the occupation, and had never had the chance to do any firefighting. Nevertheless, he received full back pay for all the time that he had been incarcerated. Apart from a couple of beatings and a week in solitary for allegedly having sniggered when a diminutive high-ranking Japanese officer tripped over his long sword while inspecting the prisoners, our new Second Engineer said he had been comparatively well treated.

Steam Tanker *Olynthus* was built in 1918 as *British Star* for British Tanker Co. Ltd. and taken over by the Admiralty in 1919. This class of ship carried 10,000 tons of fuel oil, and had a top speed of about ten knots. *Olynthus* was employed by the Admiralty as an escort oil tanker and distinguished herself as the ship which was in attendance and bunkered *Ajax*, *Exeter* and *Achilles* during the complete action at the Battle of the River Plate. Many accounts have been written about the Battle, but little credit for the successful result has been allocated to the invaluable assistance given by support ships such as *Olynthus*. Without immediate access to fuel oil it wouldn't have been possible for that particular battle to have reached a favourable conclusion. At the time the only immediate source of bunkers was *Olynthus*.

When we took the ship over from the RFA at Singapore Naval Base it was impossible to imagine Commodore Harwood and his task force having to depend on this old slow tanker to get to a specific position to provide fuel oil 'on the run' during the course of what

Binoculars used on *Olynthus* at the Battle of the River Plate. They were given to the author when he took over the vessel from the Admiralty at Singapore.

turned out to be one of the greatest sea battles. The Master and crew of *Olynthus* did some remarkable work, handling the tanker during bunkering operations in very dangerous and poor weather conditions. In 1939 there were no bow propellers or other electronic aids to keep the ships in position while oil was pumped through the line from one to another. The handling aids were limited to bridge telegraphs, underpowered steam engines and telemotor steering gear. Essentials for a specialised job such as oiling at sea were plenty of experience, good seamanship and a lot of luck. When the battleship was in Montevideo deciding what to do next, *Olynthus* received a signal from *Ajax*: 'If the Graf Spee comes your way let her through.'

British Honour, a vessel similar to the oil tanker, *Olynthus*, which was fleet oiler at the Battle of the River Plate. She was scrapped in 1960.

It took almost three months to get *Olynthus* ready for sea. A lot of work was necessary to make the ship seaworthy, including a long drydocking in Singapore. We had all had enough and just wanted to get off to sea and head home. It came to the final engine room inspection. The Chief and Second Engineers had, however, celebrated too soon and the MOT surveyor refused to sanction the issue of a Certificate of Seaworthiness until they were both in a fit condition. At the time Alan Baxter was ashore and returned on board ready to sail the ship, only to learn that the surveyor was coming back the following day to have another look at the engines – and the engineers – before clearance would be given. Baxter logged both of them for neglect of duty, and that, coming on top of an earlier logging of the Chief for being drunk at breakfast, ensured that his chances of another ship delivery job were minimal. That was the only time I ever saw a Captain log a Chief Engineer.

The ship sailed comfortably for about a week until running into the SW Monsoon crossing the Indian Ocean. With the strong winds on the beam, the ship in light ballast condition, hardly any engine power and the speed dropping to just over seven knots, the old *Olynthus* took quite a hammering, and we were relieved to reach the shelter of the Persian Gulf.

We loaded a full cargo of fuel oil in Abadan, sailed from there about the 15th of August and eventually arrived in Suez Bay ready to transit the Canal. There was a trail of black oil astern of the ship all the way up the Red Sea, and clearance for the passage through the Canal to Port Said didn't look promising. I knew nothing about it after passing out on the bridge before arriving at Suez. By the time I recovered sufficiently to take any interest we had arrived in Port Said and an Egyptian doctor was sticking a syringe into my arm. Apparently he had come on board to investigate the ship's 'Q' flag signal. He diagnosed influenza, a strange ailment to have picked up in the warm climate of the Red Sea.

However, I really knew the ship was at Port Said when a man's hand came in around the partly open door and snatched the box containing my prized first-ever Gillette razor from the compactum shelf. I did my best to jump out of the bunk and run outside. The shout of 'thief' prompted three of our Chinese crew to pick up the nearest one of a group standing nearby and throw him over the side.

After a couple of days in idyllic Mediterranean weather which continued throughout the journey all the way to Avonmouth, I was fully recovered and went back on watch. The new owner boarded as soon as we docked and saw his ship for the first time. Understandably he was very pleased with what he had got for his money. It had cost just £83,000 from the Admiralty and he was about to pocket a cheque for £80,000 freight for the cargo of oil. Not a bad bit of work as he was on the verge of selling the ship on to another Italian, which would realise even more profit.

Captain Alan Baxter asked me to stay with the ship until the cargo was discharged, and to take her West of Lundy for tank cleaning. I had been on board her for almost five months without sailing very far. That was my first oil tanker, and for some reason it proved to be the last. I must admit that when I left *Olynthus*, I was still wondering how Commodore Harwood and his mini Cruiser Squadron ever managed to win the Battle of the River Plate.

Chapter 4

Sloan's: Deep-Sea to Coasting

Beauly, *Brora*, *Findhorn*, *Annan* and *Orchy* comprised a Clyde-based fleet of cargo ships operated by William Sloan & Co. when I joined their SS *Beauly* on the 26th of December 1947 in Glasgow and sailed from the Company's berth on the Broomielaw that afternoon.

After I had spent two months ashore getting a First Mate's Certificate, the £100 pay-off from *Olynthus* had run out, and I was waiting to join another Baron Line vessel as Chief Officer. The ship wasn't due in the UK for another couple of weeks and I needed a job until then, so it was down to the Officers' Pool in James Watt Street. They had short-term vacancies on *Royal Scotsman* and *Royal Ulsterman*; both ships were employed on regular passenger services between Glasgow and Belfast. There was also a berth for a Second Mate with Sloan's. I had never heard of them and told the clerk it didn't matter which it was, but for him to choose the best. He gave me a chit for the *Beauly* and said, 'She's over on the other side of the river and sails at 5 o'clock.' I couldn't ever remember being on board a British coaster before, never mind sailing on one.

Beauly was on the Cardiff and Swansea run, calling at Belfast outward and homeward. At 4.50 p.m. Captain McGuigan walked straight off the dockside up into the wheelhouse, changed his soft hat for a uniform cap and said, 'So you're the new Second Mate. Put the engine telegraph on standby and take the wheel.' The ship left the quay in Glasgow at exactly 5.00 p.m. and I steered her down the Clyde until we passed Greenock at 7.20. I hadn't steered a ship for any length of time since my apprentice days with the Baron Line, but that part of my Home Trade initiation went fine. Coming up on the bridge at midnight in the Firth of Clyde with lights flashing all over the place and other ships sculling around, was a different matter. The Mate said, 'She's going South West by South Three Quarters South (SWxS 3/4 S) and there's a chart in the top drawer behind you if you need it. I'm going to turn in. I'll be back up at 4 o'clock. The skipper will be up sometime,' and off he went.

I had never before been on a ship's bridge in these conditions, and so close to land as well. For the first time I realised how apt the old sea-going saying was, 'Coasting men s...... themselves when they lose sight of land, and deep-sea men when they see it.' Although I had been navigation officer on several ships, they were all foreign-going. None was navigated in quarter points of the compass, only in degrees. There was always a chart on the chartroom table with the ship's position plotted on it at frequent intervals, and when we 'picked up' a shore light we called the captain. There seemed to be few similarities between Second Mate Home Trade and Second Mate Deep-sea.

Of course, I wasn't on my own on the bridge during that first watch on *Beauly*. The quartermaster and the Able Seaman who followed him at the wheel had spent many years of their sea-going careers steering coasting ships up and down the Firth of Clyde, across the Irish Sea, and throughout the Bristol Channel. I made full use of their knowledge and experience that night, but 4 o'clock couldn't come quickly enough for me all the same.

Many of Sloan's officers had been with the same company most of their working lives, starting on deck and progressing through to Chief Officer and, in some cases, Master of one of the ships. That took a very long time. Promotion was slow. The quality of the permanent officers and the standard on the ships was very high. Steady jobs on Sloan's were much sought after. The vessels were all on regular runs between Glasgow and the Bristol Channel with round trips of two weeks and good turnaround periods in the home port. I sailed on *Beauly*, *Brora* and *Annan*, and enjoyed it, but ambition didn't allow for another four or five years as Second Mate, then ten years as First Mate, before the possible chance of a Master's job.

In 1948 there were openings in every type of shipping company for officers with suitable experience and qualifications. How rapidly things changed in our once supreme shipping industry. For men wishing to carry on going to sea after the war, Sloan's was as good as a shore job. The downside for deep-sea men moving over to home trade was financial. It was a completely new lifestyle, with no big pay-offs after long trips. I asked Alec, our steward on *Beauly*, what the job was like. 'It's good,' he said, and took a half crown coin from his pocket, 'but when you look at one of these, just imagine it's a pound note.'

Beauly arrived at Donegal Quay in Belfast in time for the start of the dockers' morning shift. The cargo was loaded at a remarkably fast rate, finished in the late afternoon, and we then sailed for Cardiff. I was much more relaxed about keeping watch on the passages down through the Irish Sea and up the Bristol Channel. It was watch and watch (four on and four off) and there were now opportunities to do some proper navigation. I took full advantage of it with cross bearings, running fixes, horizontal sextant angles and even a couple of azimuths. The ship's position was displayed on the chart every hour and was left on the chart table for all to see. The others knew where the ship was at all times without it. I only knew because of it. That was another difference between deep-sea and coasting.

After a couple of days in the East Dock in Cardiff, then the South Dock Basin in Swansea, the ship sailed back up to Belfast and Glasgow. Once my first voyage was over, I reflected on the remarkably confident way in which Captain McGuigan had handled the vessel in every close-quarter situation during the two-week trip. There was no shouting and all hands were trained to do a particular task at a specific moment in the operation. Docking telegraph movements from the bridge to aft always seemed to be anticipated by the quartermaster and ABs working the ropes and fenders: my interference wasn't required. Ringing acknowledgements back up to the bridge on the docking telegraph and looking important in uniform with the ship backing stern-first in through a lock entrance wasn't too difficult, and a far cry from many deep-sea performances abroad.

The Baron boat had been delayed, so I made another trip on *Beauly*, and learned while in Cardiff that the Baron boat's arrival in the UK was imminent. I decided to forego the early promotion from Second Mate to First Mate foreign. The 'Home Trade Bug' had bitten and led to a third trip on the ship. I had discovered there was a life at

Sloan's Channel Tours.

Sloan's Channel Tours.

sea without tramping all over the world. It was a turning-point in my life. My connection with the Bristol Channel started with Sloan's in 1947 and continued one way and another for almost 50 years.

Little has ever been written about William Sloan & Company: for many years they just continued unobtrusively to supply shipping services between Scotland, Ireland, England and Wales. In the earlier days the ships carried passengers as well as cargo and probably have the distinction of getting the first ship-cruising brochure printed. It was a comprehensive guide and detailed in 70 pages every place of interest the ships passed and ports they called at during the two-week trip. It was referred to as a descriptive guide book and entitled *Scotland & North of Ireland Bristol Channel Holiday Tours*. It was published in April 1913.

Sloan's were well-established purveyors of their trade. Those who worked for them were first and foremost 'Sloan's Men'. The majority were from the Highlands and Islands of Scotland, and Gaelic was much more than a second language. I recall being stopped by one of the stevedores in the cargo shed and asked, 'And where are you from, Second Mate?' 'Glasgow,' I said, and he replied, 'But there's not many of you fellows goes to sea.' As the ship was berthed right in the centre of the City of Glasgow it may have seemed a strange remark, but having been with Sloan's long enough to know the score I added, 'But my mother is from Stornoway, my father from Ullapool, and I learned to speak Gaelic at school there.'

I was pleased to have the chance of another trip on *Beauly*. By then there were no apprehensions. My deep-sea form of navigation was accepted by the Master and First Mate. I could identify lighthouses, lightships and buoys without constant reference to Admiralty charts. Using quarter points without checking with the compass rose had become second nature. The combination of coastal and deep-sea navigation techniques was judged by all to be excellent. There were still some major differences between the two jobs. I had to pay the steward 17/6d. a week from my wage of £6 10s. to help pay for the 'grub'. The food he served up was surprisingly good, better than in some of the ships I had sailed on previously. Old seamen reading this will say, 'Of course, he worked for Hungry Hogarth.'

SS *Brora* leaving Swansea for Glasgow. *(Photo: Gareth Mills)*

In 1948, *Beauly* and *Brora* were usually on the Cardiff and Swansea run with *Orchy*, *Annan* and *Findhorn* at Bristol. *Beauly* and *Brora* were similar ships; the others were all different from them and from each other. Swansea dockers had a common name for them, the 'Bobalongs'.

Orchy was considered the flag-ship of the fleet, with the Senior Master in command. She was a fine sea-boat. That was proved in the vicinity of the tragedy when a ferry from Ireland, *Princess Victoria*, foundered in atrocious weather in the North Channel in January 1953. Sailing on *Findhorn* was quite a test of stamina and seamanship in winter conditions in the Irish Sea. Her open bridge with no wheelhouse to protect the watch-keepers from the elements meant that the 'rig of the day' was frequently oilskins, seaboots and sou'westers, with a guarantee of weatherbeaten features after a long period of service on the ship.

The first time I sailed up the seven tortuous miles of the River Avon was on Sloan's SS *Annan* and the difficulties in handling ships between Avonmouth and the Port of Bristol were only too obvious. Sloan's major casualty was SS *Ettrick* shown on the accompanying Notice to Mariners issued by the Haven Master on the 8th. of September 1924.

Wm. Sloan's SS *Ettrick* ashore and capsized at Horseshoe Bend in the River Avon.

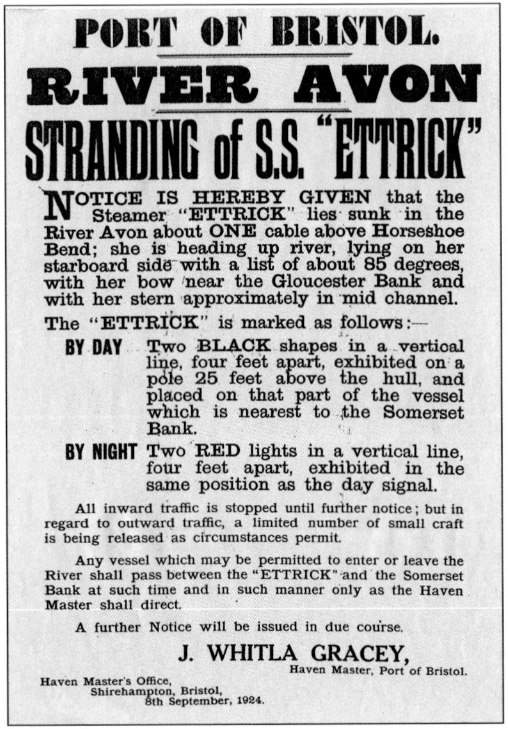

PORT OF BRISTOL.

RIVER AVON

STRANDING of S.S. "ETTRICK"

NOTICE IS HEREBY GIVEN that the Steamer "ETTRICK" lies sunk in the River Avon about ONE cable above Horseshoe Bend; she is heading up river, lying on her starboard side with a list of about 85 degrees, with her bow near the Gloucester Bank and with her stern approximately in mid channel.

The "ETTRICK" is marked as follows:—

BY DAY Two BLACK shapes in a vertical line, four feet apart, exhibited on a pole 25 feet above the hull, and placed on that part of the vessel which is nearest to the Somerset Bank.

BY NIGHT Two RED lights in a vertical line, four feet apart, exhibited in the same position as the day signal.

All inward traffic is stopped until further notice; but in regard to outward traffic, a limited number of small craft is being released as circumstances permit.

Any vessel which may be permitted to enter or leave the River shall pass between the "ETTRICK" and the Somerset Bank at such time and in such manner only as the Haven Master shall direct.

A further Notice will be issued in due course.

J. WHITLA GRACEY,
Haven Master, Port of Bristol.

Haven Master's Office,
Shirehampton, Bristol,
8th September, 1924.

CHAPTER 5 Bristol Channel Passenger Ships

From Relief Second Mate on Sloan's Glasgow & Bristol Channel cargo vessels I progressed to Mate on the *Ravenswood*, one of P&A Campbell's fine fleet of paddle-steamers which ran passenger excursion services in the Bristol Channel and on the South Coast of England. Coasting on Sloan's ships was quite a change from deep-sea tramping, but it was good preparation for handling White Funnel paddlers.

It was a specialist job, and Campbell's had very experienced men in charge of their ships. The senior officers I sailed with before being master myself were pre-war men who knew what made paddlers tick and had sailed on the ships until they were taken over for Royal Naval service when the war began. Peter and Alec Campbell, who brought the first *Waverley* down from the Clyde to try their luck in the Bristol Channel, were clearly very particular about who took charge of their ships. They were in good positions to know, as both were shipmasters themselves, as well as knowledgeable marine engineers, and had been brought up on family-owned paddle-steamers in Scotland.

Although I had been on school trips down the Clyde on the *Jeannie Deans* and a couple of others, I knew nothing about paddle-steamers, and seem to remember taking the job with Campbell's more out of

PS *Waverley*, the world's last sea-going paddle-steamer.

curiosity than anything else. At the time there were unlimited opportunities for certificated ships' officers to go wherever they wished. There was nothing further from my future seagoing ambitions than a Bristol Channel paddle-steamer. Perhaps sometimes in the years that followed I regretted it, but I never ceased to enjoy the different challenges each of the ships presented. The one similarity White Funnel paddlers had was that none was easy to handle at the piers, pontoons, and the rivers that flow into the Channel.

During 1948 I served on *Ravenswood* with Captain Lachlin McLean Shedden and was transferred to *Bristol Queen* in 1949. Going from the oldest, smallest and slowest to one of the newest, largest and fastest flagships of the company in one year was a very quick upgrade in status and, considering my lack of experience and seniority, came as a real surprise. *Ravenswood* was in many respects a small pleasure-boat trying to carry out cross-channel services without always succeeding. *Bristol Queen* was based in the home port and successfully provided steamer services throughout the Channel. This was due to the quality of the ship, the class of passenger services on board, the pick of the officers and crews, all in the charge of Captain Jack George, the best paddle-steamer master ever. 1949 was a beautiful summer, the busiest and best season during the whole time I worked on Campbell's ships in the Bristol Channel. Day after day spent working on the bridge with Jack was just the right preparation for learning how a paddle-steamer should be handled in all kinds of weather.

It was another surprise to be offered a relieving job as Master of *Glen Gower* after only two seasons as Mate. In order to get it I had to convince Bill Banks, the Managing Director, that 'it was nae trouble at all'. At the time, I even convinced myself, but it took a while to prove to older hands that I wasn't too young to do it. Just when everything seemed to be going so well for me, Jack George, who had been ill, made a speedy recovery and rejoined the *Bristol Queen*, Joe Phillips resumed command of *Glen Gower* and I spent the rest of the season as an extra Mate on *Cardiff Queen* to get time in for a Swansea licence. Between lots of studying during the long winter lay-up periods and cumulative seatime at the end of 1949 on *Bristol Queen*, I passed for Master and obtained several pilot licences for Bristol Channel ports. By the time the ships started sailing in 1950, I was fully qualified to take command of one, but had never thought it would be so soon.

Much has already been written about the ships of P&A Campbell's White Funnel Fleet and many of the personnel who sailed on them. By 1948 all the vessels were deployed on what were considered to be their most suitable stations: *Bristol Queen* on the Bristol to Ilfracombe run; *Cardiff Queen* from Cardiff down channel; *Glen Usk*, the mainstay, and the Company's breadwinner on the Cardiff to Weston Ferry, with cruises from Barry to Clevedon at low water times. *Ravenswood* was the Newport-to-Weston boat, and supplemented *Glen Usk* on the Cardiff to Weston Ferry, which was the jewel in the crown of Bristol Channel operations until the Severn Bridge interfered in 1966. *Britannia*, *Glen Gower* and *Empress Queen* completed the fleet of White Funnel ships serving the Bristol and English Channels. *Glen Gower* was based at Swansea, the other two on the South Coast. *Empress Queen*, Campbell's only turbine screw steamer, had been built for no-passport trips to France, which were denied her because of the extension of wartime regulations. She was quite unsuitable for making a living just cruising along the English Channel coast and around the Isle of Wight.

When I joined Campbell's, they were firmly back in business after the trauma of war. Twelve of their ships had gone to war; only seven had returned, two of which were scrapped as unfit for further service. The five survivors, plus the two new paddlers, *Bristol Queen* and *Cardiff Queen*, made up the UK's finest fleet of passenger excursion steamers. P&A Campbell were back in a big way.

This was reflected in more ways than one. Every Master and Chief Engineer appointed to the ships in 1948 was a pre-war experienced Bristol and English Channel man: Captain Shedden, *Ravenswood*; Joe Phillips, *Britannia*; Bert Murphy, *Glen Gower*; Findley Brander, *Glen Usk*; Jack George, *Bristol Queen*; Archie Harris, *Cardiff Queen* and Bill Couves, *Empress Queen*.

PS *Ravenswood* officers at Barry Pontoon in August 1953.
Left to right: P. Hopkins, Agent; G. Gunn, Master; J. Keating, Purser; L. Brooks, Mate; A. Campbell, Chief Engineer; Roger Whyte, Second Engineer; Reg Kenney, Chief Steward.

Balmoral (PSPS).

It was a different story with the Mates. With the exception of Jimmy Martin and Bill Watson, we were all new to the paddle-boat scene, having spent the war years and several years following the war on British merchant ships trading throughout the world. We all saw this as a home job at last.

The Campbell ships were also covered by a nucleus of pre-war pursers, senior stewards and bo'suns. As soon as the war ended, Campbell's men ashore and afloat sprouted up from all over the place and returned to their old jobs. For them, it was a return to a world with which they were thoroughly familiar. For me as a newcomer it was the start of a unique experience, as I lived and worked through the beginning to the end of the Campbell post-war empire. For me it lasted for twenty-five years. During that time I sailed as Master of all the previously mentioned ships during the first twelve years; then I

joined the Swansea Pilotage Authority as Master of their pilot vessels while waiting for the next vacancy as Harbour Pilot in the port. For the last thirteen years I carried on working for Campbells as Swansea Agent, and when I wasn't taken up with pilotage duties, as Relief Master on various ships including *St Trillo*, *Westward Ho* and *Balmoral*, which they acquired when *Cardiff Queen* and *Bristol Queen* were withdrawn from service; it was a sad end to Campbell's long and distinguished paddle-steamer services in the Bristol Channel and along the South Coast of England.

Waverley and *Balmoral*

(Reproduced with the kind permission of the Paddle-Steamer Preservation Society)

St Trillo at Llandudno.

Westward Ho at Bristol.

Ravenswood was built in 1891 for Peter and Alec Campbell, and was their first new ship after they set up a passenger excursion business in Bristol in 1887 with *Waverley*. By the time I joined *Ravenswood* as Mate in 1948, she had been continuously employed in the Bristol Channel, surviving two World Wars with the Royal Navy. After sailing for several years on foreign-going tramp steamers, I found *Ravenswood* a very different experience. Roger Whyte, our Second Engineer in 1953, had an even greater culture-shock; one of his previous vessels had been a 15,000-ton passenger liner, *Highland Brigade*; *Ravenswood* was just 345 gross tons. Long voyages on other Royal Mail Line ships were having an adverse effect on Roger's blossoming rugby career, so an Engineer's job on the little paddle-steamer, which after the War rarely ventured far away from her home base at Cardiff Pierhead, was just the job.

Roger has fond memories of his time on *Ravenswood*, which he has kindly permitted me to reproduce here:

> The chief engineer was Alec Campbell, big, bluff, good-humoured, and the black sheep of the Campbell dynasty. His father, Peter, was one of the founder brothers of the company and was unique in having not only a Master's Certificate but also a Chief Engineer's. Alec stayed with the paddlers when they were annexed by the Navy and was one of the survivors when *Glen Avon* was sunk during the Dunkirk evacuation. The ship wasn't lost through direct enemy action but foundered at anchor when the crew failed to heave it in as the weather deteriorated. Alec's luck held when a lifebuoy floated in his direction.
>
> Our hideaway during the winter was the ladies' room, which was fitted out with the most comfortable seating and a reliable, hard-working paraffin stove. We played lots of cribbage during extended lunch breaks and were regaled by Alec and Les Brooks, the Mate, with their stories of 'what it was like at sea in the old days'.
>
> The winter work for the engineers was to overhaul all machinery and prepare it for survey in the spring. The bo'sun's Mate, and Reg. Kenny, the jovial chief steward, chipped off some of the rust, and painted out the rest. Our popular purser, Jim Keating, serviced radio and electrical equipment and helped in the office, compiling advantageous sailing schedules. These fine shipmates are now with Davy Jones, but our captain, George Gunn, who was master of all six White Funnel paddle-steamers, is still going strong and spends his spare time writing about a long career in shipping. We met recently for the first time in 45 years, and as I am now one of the few Campbell's engineers still around, George has encouraged me to go into print for his new book with some reminiscences of my life 'down below' on the *Ravenswood*. The saying on ships that 'oil and water doesn't mix' may have had some credence years ago when crew members were cooped up in cramped spaces for long periods of time at sea, but didn't apply to Campbell's steamers. The officers on the three I sailed on all worked together happily and objectively.
>
> Built at Ayr in Scotland and the smallest and oldest of the fleet, *Ravenswood* had had her glory days and was always rather under-boilered and in her dotage was tired and struggling to keep up. 'Much was hoped of her, but little expected,' quoth canny George, and the sailing schedules always seemed to be drawn up with the newer, faster vessels in mind. She was always last out for Whitsun and first in (early September), a short season, which tied in nicely with my rugby commitments.
>
> On *Ravenswood* the second engineer was particularly responsible for the boiler-room. I had never sailed on a steamship and when I joined *Ravenswood* I knew as much about stoking coal fires as a householder with a poker at the hearth. I was soon to learn, and found that all too often my first job of the day was to go ashore and sign on firemen who tended to hang around Cardiff Pierhead. Some lasted no further than a solitary trip on the 'Ferry', to Weston-super-Mare and back.
>
> Alec and I soon had the main engine boxed up and ready in good time for Paddy McGrath, a wraith-like Irishman with the thickest Cardiff twang in history, and officially our nightman, to light the fires a couple of days before the ship was due to sail, to ensure that steam was slowly and carefully raised.
>
> A crew was signed on in Bristol which included a couple of firemen and a coal-trimmer; enough for the light run to Cardiff where another stokehold hand could be picked up. On Friday morning we locked out and proceeded down the Avon on the first

of the ebb at half speed; all very straightforward; but when we emerged from the confines of the river and the skipper rang 'Full Ahead' the picture suddenly changed, with the needle of the steam pressure guage soon well below the 110-lb mark with much serious shovelling, slicing, and raking needed. The trip down channel was taking much longer than expected.

The speed of the ship wasn't helped by firemen new to the shortcomings of our ancient boiler and saddled by much dross and slack in the bunkers (we were due to be coaled on arrival at Cardiff). 'Tell them to splash 'em,' the Chief kept urging; God knows what that means, I wondered. One fireman did and he set about rectifying the state of affairs caused by their burning the fires down far too early. Eventually we made it – just – on the very last of the tide and slithered up the 'Drain' to the Pierhead through little more than liquid mud. A close call indeed, and I had discovered early in my new career why our little ship was nicknamed 'The Scratcher'.

The Whitsun weather that year was poor, and passengers were few and far between, which meant quick turn-rounds at the piers and Ravenswood not disgracing herself the first week of the season. So it was in good spirits that we arrived at the Newport berth on Thursday evening for our first off-service day on Friday. One of the engineers had to remain on board the ship and it wasn't going to be Alec, who joined the rest of the crew in the rush for the Bristol train.

I found myself nervously alone on the old vessel. Two of the furnaces were drawn, the other banked up, and the diesel generator no longer required as we had to depend at night on oil lamps in our cabins. The tide was dropping and *Ravenswood* about to settle and dry out on the pontoon berth just below the town bridge. All seemed peaceful enough so I ventured ashore for a couple of pints at the Isca, the nearest pub to the ship and recommended to me as the customary 'port of call'.

Not much later I was back on board and the vessel was then high and dry; a quick peep into a deathly silent engine-room, then head down in my tiny cabin.

On *Ravenswood* the officers were accommodated in the after part of the ship below the dining-saloon; it was cosy enough and sleep came easily, but not for long, as nature called me to facilities which were up on the main deck. Armed with a company-issue torch I took another peep in the engine room and was alarmed to hear the sound of water trickling somewhere down below. *Ravenswood* was originally iron-clad but the shell plating had by then almost all been replaced by steel, some of which had worn thin enough to be unable to resist a stone which had been misplaced from the bed of the berth and penetrated one of the plates, allowing water from the rising tide to enter the bilge. Drastic emergency measures were needed so I scurried back to the cabin, found a rugby stocking, forced it into the crack and wedged it there with timber which staunched much of the ingress of water.

An early morning telephone discussion with 'Mac', the superintendent engineer, advised us to build a cement box between the frames to cover the offending crack and its stockinged plug, a task duly completed when the tide was out. We sailed like that on Saturday and for the rest of the season, when a doubler was welded over the alarmingly thin plate. There was more to Harlequins than just 'playing the game'.

On *Ravenswood*, steam and stokehold staffs were the bane of engineers' lives. Take, for example, 'Double Minehead Day' – a return trip from Cardiff in the morning, a few hours nestling on the mud at the Pierhead before floating off for the same again in the evening. But so often 'where was the steam and the firemen?' No doubt in the back bar of the Big Windsor, with no intention of turning to. On one unforgettable occasion not one fireman could be found and 300 day trippers were waiting at Minehead. On the ship's return another good crowd was expected at Cardiff for a pleasant evening cruise, so we were on the horns of a dilemma – more correctly, I was, for the stokehold was my province. I had by then learned a bit about the shoveller's art, so my assurances were accepted by relieved colleagues and off we set.

Ravenswood burned on average a ton of coal every 9 miles and Minehead (via Penarth and Barry) lay some 24 miles away. Well over 5 tons had to be trimmed from the bunkers, fed into 3 furnaces, sliced and raked, and ashes had to be dumped. My reward during the brief stop at Minehead was to run ashore and down the swiftest and most delectable couple of pints in the

SHIPS OF THE FLEET
(past and present)

Dates	Name	Length	Breadth	Gross Tonnage
Built 1885 Acqd. 1885 Dispd. 1919	WAVERLEY (I)	205.0	21.2	258 391
Built 1891 Acqd. 1891 Dispd. 1954	RAVENSWOOD	215.0	24.1	330 345
Built 1894 Acqd. 1894 Dispd. 1946	WESTWARD HO (I)	225.0	26.1	438
Built 1895 Acqd. 1895 Dispd. 1946	CAMBRIA (I)	225.0	26.1	420
Built 1896 Acqd. 1896 Dispd. 1956	BRITANNIA	230.0	26.6	459
Built 1895 Acqd. 1896 Dispd. 1903	LADY MARGARET	210.0	25.0	369
Built 1877 Acqd. 1897 Dispd. 1919	GLEN ROSA	206.1	20.0	223 296
Built 1893 Acqd. 1899 Dispd. 1919	ALBION	200.0	25.0	363
Built 1880 Acqd. 1893 Dispd. 1903	SCOTIA	211.2	21.8	260
Built 1893 Acqd. 1901 Dispd. 1902	PRINCESS MAY	160.0	21.6	260
Built 1897 Acqd. 1901 Dispd. 1915	*BRIGHTON QUEEN (I)	240.5	28.1	603 553
Built 1911 Acqd. 1911 Dispd. 1915	*LADY ISMAY	220.0	26.1	495
Built 1907 Acqd. 1910 Dispd. 1941	*BARRY/WAVERLEY(II)	225.6	26.6	471
Built 1905 Acqd. 1910 Dispd. 1940	*DEVONIA (I)	245.0	29.0	641
Built 1899 Acqd. 1910 Dispd. 1913	TINTERN	210.1	25.1	393
Built 1912 Acqd. 1912 Dispd. 1944	*GLEN AVON	220.0	27.1	509
Built 1914 Acqd. 1914 Dispd. 1963	GLEN USK	224.3	28.1	524 532
Built 1922 Acqd. 1922 Dispd. 1960	GLEN GOWER	235.1	28.5	553
Built 1905 Acqd. 1922 Dispd. 1940	*LADY MOYRA/ BRIGHTON QUEEN (II)	245.0	29.0	519
Built 1900 Acqd. 1922 Dispd. 1940	*BRIGHTON BELLE	200.0	24.1	320
Built 1896 Acqd. 1933 Dispd. 1934	DUKE OF DEVONSHIRE	175.0	20.6	257
Built 1940 Acqd. 1940 Dispd. 1955	EMPRESS QUEEN	269.5	37.5	1781
Built 1946 Acqd. 1946 Dispd. 1968	BRISTOL QUEEN	244.7	31.2	961
Built 1947 Acqd. 1947 Dispd. 1968	CARDIFF QUEEN	240.0	30.1	765
Built 1936 Acqd. 1963	ST. TRILLO	149.2	27.1	314
Built 1939 Acqd. 1965	WESTWARD HO (IV)	199.5	30.2	739

* Lost on War Service.

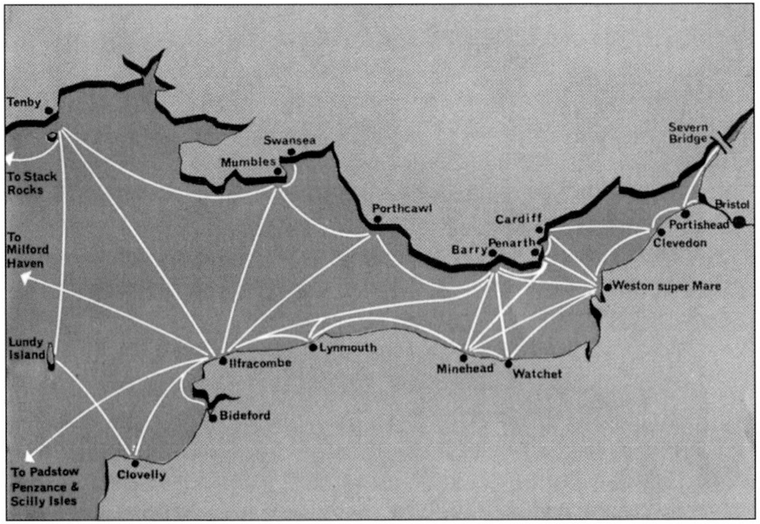

P & A Campbell's fleet-list and the courses made by the ships.

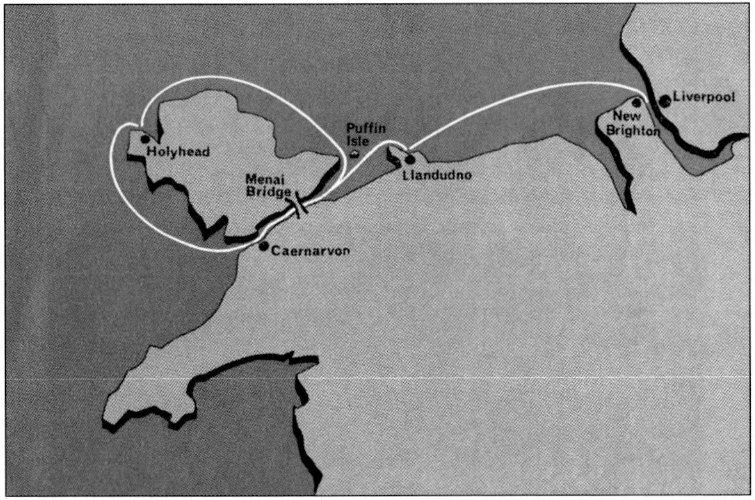

nearest harbourside pub. These were paid for with a half-crown from the takings pressed into my gnarled and blackened hand by a grateful purser.

There are memories galore, like listening on passage to Clevedon one day in Jim Keating's tiny office as Jim Laker famously took the last few of the 19 Aussie wickets to fall at Old Trafford. Alec had to cope on his own until the last wicket went down. When we had bad weather and no inroads had been made into the churn of milk which was secured to the sponson near the engine-room door I might take it below for a few days. It eventually re-emerged in the shape of a couple of pounds of pretty decent cream cheese (into which Reg. Kenny had contributed a generous dash of port wine) for our dinner table in the saloon. Cheerful evenings with Alec Campbell in his favoured pub, Little Windsor, close to the pierhead, and with the landlord, Dick Morris, himself an old sea dog, adding a generous ten pennyworth to the yarning.

The food on *Ravenswood* was generally pretty good although the catering department sometimes had trouble keeping a cook – not surprising considering the primitive galley they had to work in on board the vessel. One day, however, the bo'sun stepped into the breach and offered the services of his wife: 'She's got plenty time on her hands,' he said. We were mostly on the Cardiff-Weston ferry – three or four trips a day each way – so the bos'un's good lady obligingly came on board early each morning for a full day's work over the coal-fired stove.

She often skipped the evening trip to go home to look after her children. It turned out she had fourteen of them, including four pairs of twins. The older ones were brought up to look after the toddlers, as so often happens in large families. Jim gave them all a free outing one Sunday and what a splendid family of Cardiffian Irish they were.

George Gunn, who was our skipper in 1953, went to *Cardiff Queen* the following season, and another experienced old salt, Leo Virgo, presided over the happy team for what was to be *Ravenswood*'s 63rd and last season: she failed her MOT passenger survey and was broken up in 1955.

I was posted to *Britannia*, the greyhound of the fleet, an elegant paddle-steamer which burned oil and was able to keep time with ease. When Tommy Price, our chief engineer in 1955, retired, he was replaced by Johnny Taylor, another of the old school and a member of the Taylor family which had featured prominently in the development of the Company alongside Peter and Alec Campbell in their early days running paddle-steamers in the Bristol Channel.

Even though he had retired from the ships, Tommy Price, with whom I had first sailed on Britannia, voluntarily offered to relieve me on Saturdays so that I could be available to turn out for Harlequins. To everyone who worked with him, Tommy was a good shipmate and a very good friend.

The decline in passenger services in the Bristol Channel and on the South Coast of England resulted in the disposal of many paddle-steamers and other excursion vessels. I went into the oil business for a while before grabbing an opportunity to become a schoolmaster. P&A Campbell's White Funnel Fleet has a special place in my heart with the memories it brings of fine vessels, good shipmates and lasting friendships. 'All good things come to an end' – but not quite, as we still have *Waverley*.

I am often asked which of the six post-war paddle-steamers was the best. No two vessels were built the same and I can only give my own opinion on the merits or otherwise of each ship as I found it to be and what I can remember about some of the masters with whom I worked at the time.

Unlike many other shipping fleets, every White Funnel vessel was different in size, speed and handling propensity. This had variable effects on their performances. There were several other influences which should have been taken into consideration by the owners: engineers, firemen, and the vagaries of the Bristol Channel. When we went from one ship to another it was often a different kind of job altogether. They all had one thing in common, open bridges and no wheelhouses, and when I started there it was a controversial subject between the old and new officers. The old ones thought that a Bristol Channel paddle-steamer couldn't operate safely when those on the bridge didn't have a decent all-round view. The new Mates were used to being enclosed from the weather and didn't agree; I had experienced both and couldn't have cared less, but I was young and liked fresh air.

Easily the most popular ship with my older contemporaries was *Britannia*. As far as Jack George, Brander, Harries and Bert Murphy were concerned, she was still the flagship created by the Campbells and they didn't intend it to change. Unlike *Bristol Queen* and *Cardiff Queen* the '*Brit.*' wasn't designed for anything but speed and ease of handling, which of course accounted for her popularity, but not always with passengers in heavy weather, as I found out during my six weeks with her on the 'Swansea Run'in 1953. Findlay Brander was on the ship when her boiler blew up. He was transferred to *Glen Usk* and took his allegiance with him: *Glen Usk* suddenly became 'the best ship in the Company' as long as she was kept on the Cardiff/Weston ferry, as all the way down to Ilfracombe was bad for the wee ship, and for Findlay himself.

I very much enjoyed working on every ship I sailed on in the fleet and with all officers and members of the crews. There was a 'good shipmate' feeling ashore and afloat which I had never experienced before. Joining Campbell's in 1948 was like taking part in a post-war family reunion. Having been initiated into Bristol Channel paddlers on *Ravenswood* has some effect on my choice of ships.

Ravenswood was well ahead of the others. *Cardiff Queen* had the best bridge for handling the ship in poor weather conditions, was comfortable for crews and liked by passengers. *Britannia* was very fast and the easiest to handle in compatible weather conditions, but uncomfortable in moderate to heavy beam seas. The best job in the company was having *Britannia* on a nice quiet Bristol or Cardiff sailing down channel in the lee of the North Devon coast. *Bristol Queen* was the most spacious, and easily the best sea boat, but I never felt really comfortable with the bridge. Perhaps another six inches on my height would have helped. *Glen Usk* was the most reliable on the Ferry, with the best record at Weston Pier – the most difficult place in the Channel to get a ship alongside. As with Brander, Leo Virgo who took over from him, liked the ship and the Ferry. Few others did.

PS *Cambria* ashore on Rillage Point near Ilfracombe.

Cambria's passengers waiting for transport back to Ilfracombe.

Cardiff Queen.

Britannia.

Bristol Queen.

Glen Gower.

The engines inherited by *Glen Gower* when the old *Albion* was scrapped didn't help her speed and helm movements. She was the most awkward of the ships to handle, but if passengers weren't in any hurry to get there, it was usually a comfortable enough trip. Every ship has its own characteristics: to *Glen Gower*'s credit she was probably the most traditional-looking paddle steamer Campbell's ever built.

After a few years spent working on Campbell's ships, it became quite clear there was a very limited future for young officers in the Company. As my next real ambition was to be a ship's pilot, I made a successful application for a job as Harbour Pilot in the Port of Swansea; we moved down there from Bristol in 1957 and I continued as master of *Cardiff Queen* for another couple of years, then worked as skipper on the Pilot vessels, *Roger Beck*, *Woodbridge*, then on the new ship, *Seamark*, when she came into service. As I write, *Seamark* is being taken out of service after 40 years spent embarking and disembarking pilots on ships in the Bristol Channel. In the late 1950s the Port of Swansea employed 24 Sea Pilots and 15 Harbour Pilots. During my twelve years as Harbour Pilot I docked, sailed or shifted an estimated 3000+ vessels: Swansea was a busy port. Concurrently with pilotage duties I looked after Campbell's business ashore as agent and relief master on their ships. In 1973 I resigned from the pilotage and transferred to Dover as Assistant Marine Superintendent with Townsend Car Ferries which, like Campbell, had become part of the European Ferries Group of companies. Another latent desire was satisfied.

There were many other shipmates on Campbell's ships with whom it was a pleasure to sail but the officers on *Ravenswood* in 1953 were collectively the best. The fact that the only three motor cars in the Company were owned by my officers on *Ravenswood* is quite coincidental.

Chapter 6

Bristol Channel Pilotage

Ship's pilotage covers a very wide range of different services to vessels all over the world. I was a harbour pilot for twelve years in the port of Swansea and, leading up to that, master of pilot vessels in the Bristol Channel for three years. It isn't possible now to estimate accurately how many acts of pilotage I did during that time, but it is unlikely to have been fewer than 3000. Most of the pilots I worked with stayed in the job until retirement age; I went from Swansea to European Ferries in Dover, the shipping group which acquired P&A Campbell with whom I had sailed before joining Swansea Pilotage Authority. I could write at length about piloting and the large variety of ships which docked, shifted, and sailed from a port like Swansea which handled up to eleven millions tons a year, but I'll content myself with noting only a few interesting memories.

In 1969, I had the pleasure of berthing HMS *Glamorgan* when the warship brought Prince Charles to Swansea after his Investiture as Prince of Wales at Caernarfon. The ship tied up at the berth about 11.30 a.m. and the Captain went ashore for a civic reception. He instructed the ship's surgeon to look after the pilot. I followed him down to the wardroom, which was well filled with officers waiting for 'the sun to get over the yardarm' at noon. The doctor said to the assembly, 'Although the sun hasn't quite made it yet, gentlemen, we have a guest on board which makes it permissible to open the bar, and, by the way, the drinks are all on the Yanks; remember it's the 4th of July, Independence Day, and we don't want them to celebrate on their own. There were a number of American naval officers on board under NATO exchange agreements between the two countries. They also decided to drink a few toasts to Prince Charles, and by then nobody seemed to care who was paying. Luckily I didn't have any more ships to attend to on that tide.

Apart from certain special classes of ship such as those carrying passengers, vessels entering, leaving or shifting around in the port were not compelled to take a pilot. We Harbour Pilots had differing opinions as to whether or not it was to our advantage. As long as we were informed in advance by agents what was required, there were no problems. That didn't always happen, as some of the agents we dealt with didn't discourage ship's masters from doing the job themselves, unless, of course, the conditions were bad and there was a chance that the ship might not want to dock or sail on its own. The owners were usually aware that it was not necessary for them to carry a pilot, and of course they almost always didn't, for obvious economic reasons.

One unusual experience that I had was when I was misinformed that a small Dutch vessel wanted a pilot to shift to another dock, so I went with the Harbour Boatmen to do the job. The Captain asked who I was and I told him that I was the pilot. He said that his owners didn't allow him to take pilots in non-compulsory ports and he was likely to get fired if he did. This Captain didn't seem to be very highly regarded by his boss. I asked if he knew where he had to go with the ship. He didn't and offered me £1 and a bottle of whisky to take him there as that wouldn't show up on his accounts. It didn't show up on ours, either, as I kept the pound and shared the whisky with the rest of the watch. The total bill in 1962 for a harbour pilotage movement such as that was one pound eighteen and six (£1 18s 6d) so in some respects it balanced out.

Greek ships were probably the most frequent foreign visitors to the port. They came in all shapes and sizes and we pilots all had our fair share of stories to tell about them. I thought by the look of her when I went on board at three in the morning that one vessel was owned and operated by Greeks. When the captain told me that they had left Milford Haven five days before, I knew she was. The weather wasn't good, and like the ship itself he looked the worse for wear. Milford is just sixty-five miles from Swansea.

The coal hoist at which the ship eventually berthed was just across the dock from the lock gates, and I didn't get off her until five thirty, two and a half hours after going on board. The usual time from lock to coal hoist was about half an hour. The captain hadn't been off the bridge since the ship left Milford. I made one tug fast aft and the crew didn't know how to let it go. There was no way of communicating with anyone except the captain and when I had to leave the bridge to let the rope go myself I gave him my pea-whistle and told him to sound it if anything more than imminent misfortune was likely. It was still blowing a gale and pouring down with rain. After the two-and-a-half-hour saga I accepted the usual invitation extended by all good ship's masters to pilots. On this occasion it was willingly accepted and gratefully received; luckily I knew what it was without being able to see through a rather opaque tumbler.

I asked him why the ship was registered in Famagusta. He said, 'Mr Pilot, it is a flag of convenience so that we don't have to keep the ship up to Greek standards.'

There were usually more memorable events on small ships than on the large ones. One night, late on tide, I was called out to sail a foreign coastal tanker from the oil terminal. I went straight to the bridge as the Lock Master was shouting on the VHF, 'Take the ship down right away or she'll miss the tide. We can fit her in ahead of a large vessel, and that will be it.'

I asked the person in the wheelhouse if the engines were ready. He said that they were, as it was direct control from bridge to engine room. I told the ropemen on the jetty to let everything go, took the wheel and worked the ship through from there into the lock ahead of the other vessel and its tugs. The lock was running down, and it was time to get off. I asked, 'Captain, will you please sign my bill?' The person who had helped me get the ship down to the lock said, 'I'm the Mate, not the Captain.'

Before I could leave the wheelhouse the Captain burst in and shouted, 'Where the hell are we?'

I said, 'In the lock and the gates are about to open.'

'But I don't want to sail; the weather's too bad.'

I decided to get off the ship as quickly as possible without bothering about his signature on the bill. The Sea Pilot was on his way up to the bridge and the ship was being called out of the lock. She had to get out and there was no way back. The tide was over, the weather outside was dreadful, and the young lady he had been entertaining didn't have time to dress and get ashore. The Sea Pilot told me later that the Captain had been asleep in his bunk and hadn't known that his ship had sailed until it was too late. The vessel was bound for Liverpool and no doubt the Captain's guest had to find her own way back to Swansea. I never lived it down.

Piloting in Swansea in the '60s and '70s was a good, secure job. Perhaps it was the security and the routine which went with it that motivated me to accept the offer from European Ferries and move down to Dover. There were another fifteen years or so to go before retiring and there still seemed many more interesting things to do in life before that came round although I must admit I didn't expect what came next to be quite as interesting and challenging as it all turned out to be.

CHAPTER 7

English Channel Ferries

It was in Dover that Townsend Car Ferries started what is now the busiest cross-channel passenger/vehicle service in the world. Their first ship, *Artificer*, carried just fifteen cars, which were loaded and unloaded by crane at both Dover and Calais. The vessel's certificate allowed only twelve persons to accompany the cars and any in excess of that had to travel across the Channel on a separate passenger ship and rejoin their vehicles at the other end.

With the increasing traffic between England and France, *Artificer* was replaced by *Royal Firth*, and she in turn by *Forde*, which operated until the outbreak of war in 1939. After government service, *Forde* resumed sevice on the Dover/Calais run until she was replaced in 1950 by *Halladale*. Cranes were used to load and unload the cars from the ship until the first roll-on, roll-off ramp was built at Calais in 1951.

The first new *Free Enterprise* ship came into service in 1951, and she was quickly followed by six more modern drive-through *Free Enterprise* named vessels.

Before a marine superintendency was established at Dover itself, the complete operation of the ships was controlled from London. The Group was rapidly expanding, with an extensive new ferry-building programme and the acquisition of P&A Campbell's White Funnel Fleet, and Stanhope Steamship Company, in addition to Atlantic Steam Navigation's ships and ferry services from the UK to Ireland and the Continent. Despite stiff opposition from the then Labour Government, European Group, as it now called itself, won the right to acquire the port of Felixstowe and developed it to be one of the UK's major container terminals. An attempt to buy out British Rail Shipping's fleet of forty passenger vessels was disallowed by a government commission, and instead of them going to a 100% British-owned group they were unfortunately allowed to be sold to foreign interests, which seemed utterly senseless to me.

During my time with Townsend they operated eight ships from Dover, sailing regularly to Calais and Zeebrugge: *Free Enterprise 1*-*V11* and *Autocarrier*. That ship, better known as *Royal Sovereign*, was built in 1948 for passenger excursions and converted by Townsend in 1967 to carry cars and freight. She was the trailblazer of the Dover to Zeebrugge service and wasn't expected to do much, just to get over and back as soon as possible. There was no suitable berth for *Autocarrier* at Zeebrugge so, when the ship was due, a pontoon was towed into the lock at the entrance to the Canal and vehicles driven off on to the quayside.

Under the circumstances, *Autocarrier* did a great job, but with new developments and modern requirements for ferries, she became redundant and was sold to Italian owners. Although I worked with *Autocarrier* for only a short time, I had great respect for what the ship, officers and crews accomplished under indifferent circumstances and conditions, and it was sad to see her go. It was even sadder afterwards to hear the Italians had put her ashore and that the ship was therefore a total loss.

Free Enterprise I was an attractive little ship and had much to do with the successful development of the standards attained by today's operatives of short-sea car ferries. I would never support any criticism or detrimental comments regarding the ship and tried to ensure, sometimes 'against the tide', that *FE I* was given the same care and attention as was lavished on the newer vessels.

Free Enterprise I	was eventually sold to the Greeks.
Free Enterprise II	went to Italy.
Free Enterprise III	went to Saudi Arabia.
Free Enterprise IV	and *Free Enterprise VI* went to Egypt.
Free Enterprise V	went to British owners.
Free Enterprise VII	had a major conversion from almost 5000 GRT to more then 12000 GRT and was renamed *Pride of Rathlin*.

The car ferry, *Halladale*, leaving Dover for Calais.

Free Enterprise I.

By 1974 the Company, now known as Townsend Thoresen, a part of the European Ferries Group, owned the best fleet of short-sea passenger ships sailing out of Dover. They benefited from the meteoric rise which took place after the war in cross-channel passenger, car, and freight transportation, and took action earlier than most other operators to build the right vessels for the job. The business acumen of former managing director Roland Wickenden and the technical skill of Jim Ayers, naval architect, created a practical and comfortable fleet of ships.

Innovative construction ideas such as drive-through arrangements for vehicles and 'walk-through' access for passengers from wide, centrally-situated stairways, allowed for bars, shops, and other facilities to be sited and easily available right along both sides of the vessels' lounges. For many passengers, finding their way when on board a ship, particularly on short passages, can be confusing when they continually have to look round corners. The introduction of an open-plan design reduced that problem.

The ships were good and the officers on them excellent. That was my first impression on arriving in Dover in 1973, even though there was very little standardisation on board the ships. Each one was under the direct control of a Senior Master and Senior Chief Engineer. In the absence of a shore superintendency at Dover, the operation of each ship reflected the ideas of individuals rather than company policy as a whole. There was no shortage of new suggestions percolating down from what was sometimes referred to on the ships as 'the dream factory in London'. How or whether they could or would be used to advantage seemed to be a matter of personal choice. For example, until then each vessel had its own ideas on how directional signs for passengers should be used. This, a most important feature on short-sea passenger-carrying vessels, was just another priority to be attended to.

Soon after starting work at Dover I was called out during the night. *Free Enterprise I* had struck an 'unidentified underwater object at Calais and was sinking'. It had happened at the harbour entrance and although the engine room was filling up with water the master and crew had managed to get the ship into a berth and disembark the passengers and vehicles with some difficulty, but safely. Luckily, a vessel due to drydock at Calais had been delayed by bad weather because there was nowhere else for *FEI* to go. The ship was towed across to the drydock and when I arrived in the early hours she was on the blocks with water pouring out from a large hole in the bottom shell plating. The engine room was completely submerged up to deck level and the Chairman of the Chamber of Commerce and representatives of the tug-boat company were waiting for me in the Captain's cabin. During the critical time, and with the ship moored alongside the berth, they had tried unsuccessfully to get the Master to sign Lloyd's Open Salvage Form. The Master refused to do so, saying it was just a short tow from the berth to the drydock. Pressure was put on the Townsend Agent, who telephoned the Managing Director in Dover, who instructed him to get the Master to sign the form. I fully supported the Captain's refusal. Under the circumstances only he can make that decision and no amount of coercion, for whatever reason, can affect it.

Several times the towage costs were agreed for moving the ship from berth to drydock. Many harsh words were spoken in English and French and there was a serious breach of the *entente cordiale*. Some time later I attempted my own reconciliation when I entertained the Calais Harbour Master and members of his Chamber of Commerce to lunch at the White Cliffs Hotel in Dover.

My orders from London, through the Chief Superintendent, were to 'ensure that this Master must never be in charge of one of our ships again'. I said that this was quite unacceptable, as he would have to take full responsibility for the incident without recourse to a proper investigation.

Our inspection into the cause of the accident identified the obstruction as an uncharted concrete section of the breakwater foundation encroaching on the approach channel. Responsibility for the construction of harbour charts and plans rested with Calais Port Authority, and, of course, with their Chamber of Commerce. All the ship's engines and auxiliaries were stripped down, and the vessel was off service in Flushing for about twelve months; it was very rewarding to have ensured that the Master would continue to be in charge of one of our ships.

The whole episode seemed to suggest that the shipping company was prepared to jeopardize the captain's position in order to maintain good working relations with Calais Harbour Authority.

Another incident with similar implications happened at Zeebrugge. *Free Enterprise VII* also struck an unidentified underwater object when she was approaching the berth. A large area of bottom plating was set in and the inference was that the ship had strayed outside the buoyed channel. The Master firmly denied it. After initial enquiries had been made, I felt this was another case in which the Captain of the ship would be made the scapegoat unless a full survey of the harbour was carried out. I engaged a Dutch salvage company, which sent one of their well-equipped vessels to Zeebrugge. Although we got a good sonar echo right at the spot where the master said the ship had struck, the Belgians wouldn't allow a diver to go down and told us to cease work and leave Zeebrugge immediately. Our suspicions were confirmed.

The extent of the investigation into this incident was met with little support or enthusiasm from my superiors in Dover, and questions were asked about the time and expense incurred. My very full report to the underwriters was used at an enquiry held in Belgium. Some time after I left Townsend, Captain Tony Hackett sent me a letter of thanks in which he said that 'the case was decided in our favour'.

The Dutch salvage company came to our assistance several times, usually to free mooring wires picked up by a ship's propellers or rudders. Every job undertaken was quick and efficient. In all departments of marine salvage the Dutch have no real competitors.

Free Enterprise V lost an anchor when the ship was somewhere abeam of Ostend. The port anchor and several lengths of cable had run out with the ship underway between Zeebrugge and Dover. The crew had slipped the chain and, in accordance with the procedures recommended in *Nicholl's Seamanship and Nautical Knowledge*, had marked the position with a lifebuoy tied to the end of the chain by a length of small rope. Captain Blowers had plotted an excellent Decca fix on his chart. The weather was fine and it was a perfect scenario for retrieving lost anchors, or so it seemed when I arrived in the office and was told of the incident.

There were no safety problems and the vessel wasn't damaged. The main consideration was to keep her in service. As she was likely to be running for only a short while with one anchor the MOT surveyor approved a limited dispensation.

I got in touch with our Dutch friends in Flushing and gave them the details. We agreed on 'no cure, no pay' and a cost for the job based on an estimated weight of the anchor and cable. It was looking good until the Chief Superintendent was advised by another staff member that he knew a local man at Folkestone with the right ship and equipment who would salvage the anchor for half the price. My arrangements with Flushing were immediately cancelled.

I was kept informed by RT from our two vessels on the Zeebrugge run about the Folkestone man's progress. All was going well until the diver failed to shackle the lifting wire onto the anchor cable. It wouldn't have mattered if he hadn't disconnected the buoy rope first. They had to start again from scratch to find the anchor and the ship had to shelter at Ostend from bad weather. They tried for several more days after the weather had improved but still couldn't find the anchor, and had to return to Folkestone as they were running out of fuel and stores. The MOT surveyor's patience was also running out, and he gave me an ultimatum: the ship would have to get another anchor immediately or be taken off service. I got in touch with Flushing and they agreed to take over the job. Two days later I received a call from them: they had picked up the anchor and cable and it was available for identification. Captain Craig, who had been master of *FEI* during the 1973 Calais incident, went to Flushing, checked it out and arranged for it to be put on board *FEV* at Zeebrugge.

A few months later, during a night out at Ostend, I asked the English manager of the salvage company how they had retrieved the anchor so easily. He said, 'You don't give a Dutch salvage outfit a good Decca position of anything and expect them to stay in port while someone else does the job.' The *Free Enterprise V* anchor and cable had been in their yard at Flushing all the time.

The *Herald of Free Enterprise*, which was tragically overturned off Zeebrugge, resulting in the loss of a distressingly large number of lives.

The Folkestone man arrived at my office with a bill for £500 disappointment payment. I suggested he try elsewhere.

It's very strange how often anchor and windlass troubles occur just after a ship has been in drydock. This one had recently been refitted at Brigham & Cowans (affectionately known to sailors all over the world as Break'em & Smash'em). We had experienced a similar problem with *Baron Renfrew* in Belfast Lough during the War. She had just left drydock after a major overhaul. Oh yes! Once again it had been old Brigham & Cowans in South Shields.

The anchor and cable salvage was another example of trying to do things on the cheap. Like many other problems of this nature that I have seen in many years of sailing and handling ships, it is ultimately more expensive. Unfortunately the final decision isn't always an experienced one.

In the case of *Sea Empress*, which went ashore on the Pembrokeshire coast, there was a mixture of everything. Proper powerful salvage tugs should have been called as soon as the ship looked to be in trouble. Harbour tugs are useless with a vessel of that size, particularly in the weather and tidal conditions which prevailed at the time. My immediate thoughts were, 'If they get the Dutch, she's in with a good chance.' Sadly, many people will live with the after-effects of a disaster which could have been minimised or even prevented.

Car ferry operation at Dover was a very intensive business for all concerned. The vessels were allowed only 1¼ hours alongside a RoRo berth and then had to clear out to make way for other ships standing by to take their place. During that short period of time anything up to 900 or 1200 passengers and cars, caravans, coaches and freight vehicles had to be discharged and another load shipped. Concurrently, the vessels took on board stores, bunkers, water, and replenished passenger meals and duty-free goods. Periodic crew changes were also made. It was all 'come and go' twenty-four hours a day.

I never regretted accepting the job as Nautical Superintendent of Townsend Ferries, but neither did I regret leaving them. Following on twelve years as Master of Bristol and English Channel passenger vessels and another twelve years as a Swansea Harbour Pilot, working as a ships' superintendent in Dover was another of life's interesting and exciting experiences, which by then I was getting quite used to, and without which there wouldn't now be so much to write about.

CHAPTER 8

UK, Greece, Canada & Great Lakes

The group policy adopted by European Ferries – to replace nautical superintendents with engineers and transfer to them the title of Marine Superintendent – could have been thought up only by accountants and others with little or no knowledge of how to run ships. Unfortunately, this was a creeping disease in London which found its way down to Dover during my time there with Townsend's. Economy had replaced safety and efficiency: this much was obvious on board ship if not ashore. It was justified by the advancements in electronic navigation. Traditions in British merchant shipping were abandoned in favour of cost-cutting convenience, and they never came back. As can be imagined, that didn't go down well with traditional seamen, who favoured safety before economy. British merchant shipping as we knew it was bound for extinction. With that in mind, I refused all alternative positions offered within the group and decided to have my contract settled with European Ferries.

As I had had lots of nautical experience and overseen refits, repairs, drydockings and maintenance on Townsend vessels, it was time to go it alone and set up as a ship's consultant. That happened to coincide with an advert, by a well-established American company specialising in corrosion control on bulk carriers, oil tankers and drilling rigs, for a technical representative to manage their business in the UK and to work when necessary in Holland, Belgium, France and Greece. It was a good opportunity to get a new career off the ground, and to all intents and purposes I became a marine consultant working from home. Dover was an excellent position, close to the Continent and just a couple of hours by rail from London (when the trains were running). Clearkin was a private company based in Philadelphia and the forerunner of corrosion control on oil rigs in the USA. It was also involved world-wide with VLCCs (very large crude carriers).

My new career started off well, with an annual retainer which compared favourably with the Townsend salary, an American Express card on the company's Philadelphia account, and an international flightcard for use on any airline. It was a very generous package for the job and a better start could never have been imagined. Most of their European business was conducted from Rotterdam, where (with the exception of London), I spent most of my time. I soon got used to working for Americans and enjoyed it right from the start. Oil exploration in the North Sea was well under way and production had started. Working on drill rigs was a new and exciting experience. It took place off Aberdeen, at Nigg Bay in the North of Scotland, and at Lamlash Bay in the Isle of Arran. The necessity to be fit and reasonably agile was well tested, challenging, but very rewarding. Almost all my work was down below inside the sponsor ballast tanks of the semi-immersible rigs. I found all other work in corrosion control on ships was relatively easy and a lot safer.

During the years in Swansea I had piloted more Greek ships than any other foreign vessels. The majority were unpopular 'rust buckets' and often a pilot's nightmare to handle. When I became a marine consultant specialising in corrosion control, my feelings about the condition of Greek ships suddenly changed and I looked forward to getting on board as many as possible.

A couple of weeks in Athens and Piraeus gave me a real insight into Greek ships and their owners, with whom all dealings were made. I learned a lot in those two weeks, in particular, not to rent a car in Athens and drive it yourself. My first one was delivered to the hotel and ran out of petrol en route to a gas station less than 500 yards away. The second one broke down in Syntagma Square in the centre of Athens during the rush hour which starts at 6.00 a.m. and lasts until midnight. I abandoned the third car at a car park in Piraeus.

Before my second trip to Greece it was clearly necessary to have somewhere to work from, so I made an arrangement with a company I knew in London. They had an office on the harbour front in the centre of the shipping fraternity, and an English secretary with lots of experience in shipping and also of the Greek way of life. The one turned out to be just as important as the other. At that time Greece was one of the world's three largest shipowning countries. In Piraeus alone there were more than 1000 registered shipping companies.

For the next three years I made annual trips to Greece; the Greek people I dealt with were friendly and there were no problems in making the right business contacts. There was a very large British community, most of them connected to the shipping business one way or another, so that not only my work but also my social life in Athens and Piraeus was very pleasant. The hotel at which I stayed was close to Athens Golf Club and, after I was introduced by the hotel manager, my regular weekly game continued. I later received a letter from the Club with an invitation to play in the 'International Amateur Golf Championship of Greece' which was gratefully accepted. The next three visits were increased from two to three weeks, one for golf, one for work and then a boat to the offshore islands for peace and quiet.

Mixing business with pleasure was a highly recommended practice in Greece, and I did everything possible to adhere to this national tradition. Although some of my work there could entail ship inspections, it mainly involved meeting with owners or their superintendents about future business. There were sufficient shipping offices in Piraeus for hourly appointments to be made by our secretary. Owing to a national disinclination for midday work, mornings and evenings were prime times to consult and I enthusiastically observed the tradition and helped to swell the numbers of British expats who filled the Marine Club on the quay between one and four every day but Sunday.

My connections with Greek ships were not confined to their home country, as many had offices in London as well as Piraeus and Athens. On several occasions I met with the same company representatives in both places, and despite not always getting all the business I wanted, made lots of friends in the Greek shipping communities. When I later took over as manager of Bolton Shipping Company's Marine Services in London I was very grateful to have so many friends and good connections in London and in Greece.

Although I had a good deal of experience of driving in Europe and elsewhere, I admit to having chickened out in Athens, and on the annual visits used taxicabs wherever I had to go. There were hundreds of cabs, their drivers all shouting at someone or other and blowing their horns at the same time. For courtesy and other reasons there were some practices which had to be observed and accepted by the cab passenger: *As soon as the car starts moving get a good firm grip on the safety bar which stretches across the cab behind the driver's seat, and don't be surprised if, some time after getting in, you find yourself further away from where you intended to go than when you started. During that time other passengers will probably be picked up to share the cab, although they are all likely to be dropped off before you. The taxi driver will have to charge you the full fare with intermediate (personal) contributions from your fellow travellers.* There was the time when a cab's tyres blew out at night on the main road between Piraeus and Athens. As the driver started to wrestle with the spare in the boot I suggested to my colleague, Alan, we hail another taxi. His reply was, 'We'll give him a hand instead; we know here there's at least one good tyre on this car.'

On each of the three years I took part in the annual golf tournament at Glyfada, my wife accompanied me and helped the UK players in many ways during the competitions. On two occasions the Championship Cup as well as the Team Trophy went to the UK, and I really have to say that the most enjoyable golf I ever played in sixty years was in Greece.

In Greece the Marine Club at Piraeus was the focal point for the initiation of shipping business arrangements. In London it was the Institute of Marine Engineers' Club, right in the centre of the city. I learned early on that trudging around London calling at offices was a complete waste of time. Shipping company superintendents and others involved with technical operations were fully aware that they could get whoever they required through the Institute and at the same time enjoy a nice convivial lunch break with friends. Membership of the Engineers' Club had an influence on my future.

The Marriott Company in the USA had by that time started building, in various overseas countries, hotels, which they then taught the locals how to run. Owing to unavoidable delays, their contract to build an hotel in Kuwait came unstuck and couldn't be completed in time to meet the Sheik's impatient requirements, so they agreed to convert a large passenger vessel, take it to Kuwait and sink it to the bottom adjacent to a proposed leisure-complex ashore. By coincidence Marriott owned just the right ship which had been taken out of service and laid up in Greece (where else?).

Gordon Fraser, a marine architect and a member of the Institute, was commissioned to estimate the stability requirements to position the ship permanently on the bottom of the berth in Kuwait. It was quite a complex job, and, as he was a marine engineer, one of the conditions in the contract was that a Master Mariner had to be involved. I was pleased to take on the job.

The ship was moved from Greece to Rijika in Yugoslavia and Gordon invested in a computer for the eventual calculations. We flew out to Yugoslavia and commenced work. Luckily, I had plenty of recent experience of crawling through ships' ballast tanks and we spent two uncomfortable weeks doing just that; it was the middle of summer and very hot indeed, especially down below with the confined conditions inside the bottom of the ship where there were dozens of small compartments. All US passenger vessels were built for use in wartime and no expense was spared in doing so.

It was the first time I had worked in a Yugoslavian shipyard. British yards were frequently criticised for late delivery and indifferent workmanship, but by comparison with Rijeka they had nothing to fear. Gordon and I started work every day at 7.00 a.m. and carried on right through until 6.00 p.m., then back to the hotel in Opatija for dinner about 7.30. The shipyard workers also started at 7.00 then knocked off for an hour's breakfast break at 8.00 and were home and changed and out for a stroll with their wives and families by 3.00 p.m. at the latest. There was no chance of any more work that day. The ship got to Kuwait one year late, but 'took the bottom' perfectly.

By then, Bolton Shipping Group, one of the few remaining privately owned companies left in the UK, had started up a marine services section and I was invited to join as manager based at their offices in the Corn Exchange Building near the Institute. Bolton ran a number of bulk carriers trading worldwide and had many other interests in and outside the shipping industry.

I joined Bolton just in time to feel the full force of the outcome to Mrs Thatcher's battles with coal miners and trade unions, which had brought about the 'Winter of Discontent'. Until then there had been no problems with living in Dover and working in London, as long as I left early enough in the morning and didn't care what time I got back home in the evening. However, train services got so bad that when I left home there was no guarantee of getting back the same day. Eventually, we decided to move to Windsor. While I was working with Bolton my business trips to Greece continued. At that time there were some well-founded suspicions that in various ways and for similar reasons owners and other interested parties were deliberately getting rid of ships. Events have proved that Greek shipowners and ship masters were much more skilled than anyone else at scuttling uneconomic tonnage. In legal terms, such acts as those are called barratry, and the major talking point in 1979/80 when I was in Greece was a supertanker named *Salem* which came unstuck for a number of reasons. However, it shouldn't be presumed that it was only Greek owners who were interested in losing ships at sea for financial gain.

During the winter of 1951/52, when all Campbell's paddlers were laid up, I had been offered a temporary job as Master of a small cargo vessel trading between the UK and the Continent. It fitted in quite well as long as I was available for the start of the season in the Bristol Channel. I met the owner in Cardiff, and he took me down to Port Talbot where the ship was loading for Belgium.

The Salvage Surveyor was on board inspecting some damage from the previous trip. After we had had a look round the ship the owner invited both of us to go ashore for lunch. We went to the Grand Hotel, which at that time was a pleasant place to eat. Our host passed the menu round. Although food supplies hadn't improved, and rationing was still the order of the day, we had the best the Grand could dish up, whatever the cost. The bill duly arrived, and he scanned it carefully before passing it to the surveyor and saying, 'Take that out of your expenses.'

Drakedene.

I wondered what other surprises were in store. By the time some of them surfaced, the ship was at sea. Unfortunately, before he had gone ashore the owner had picked up the radio in my cabin and taken it with him, saying, ‘You won’t need this, it’s mine; you should be able to get weather forecasts without it.’ I found this rather strange as well. I had one Mate, an engineer and a greaser, two deckhands, a steward/cook and a boy. It wasn’t bad for a vessel of that size and some of them, including the Mate, having sailed on the ship before, seemed quite happy with their lot. Nevertheless, I hoped my first impressions had been wrong.

We arrived at Ghent at Easter, the coal was discharged and I took the ship over to another berth to load general cargo for the UK. There was another surprise in store for me. The ship’s agent asked if I had yet received any wages. I said that I hadn’t, but it would be included in the accounts on the portage bill and settled with the owners when the vessel docked in the UK. He indicated that I would be lucky to get paid at all and should do something to cover myself before we got to a home port. Wristwatches were almost unobtainable in Britain, but Belgium had them coming through from Switzerland, so he brought me six to sell in the UK. They would go through his accounts, which wouldn’t arrive in Cardiff until after the ship docked, and which had to be honoured immediately.

We sailed from Belgium with general cargo for Swansea and Cardiff and a sufficient number of watches to cover any deficiency in my salary. The ship arrived in Roath Dock in Cardiff on Sunday; I smuggled the watches through an unmanned gate into the Splott district of the port, caught a train home to Bristol and got back on board on Monday morning. Despite two calls at the office in Bute Street I didn’t manage to see the owner. I was told that he was on business elsewhere, but that if I left the accounts they would be settled when the ship got to Swansea. I got the ship to Swansea, and while she was loading patent fuel at the Graigola Wharf I went to Cardiff for the money. The owner said he hadn’t had time to go through the accounts, but it would all be done by the time the ship got to Liverpool. I said that unless I was paid immediately she would have

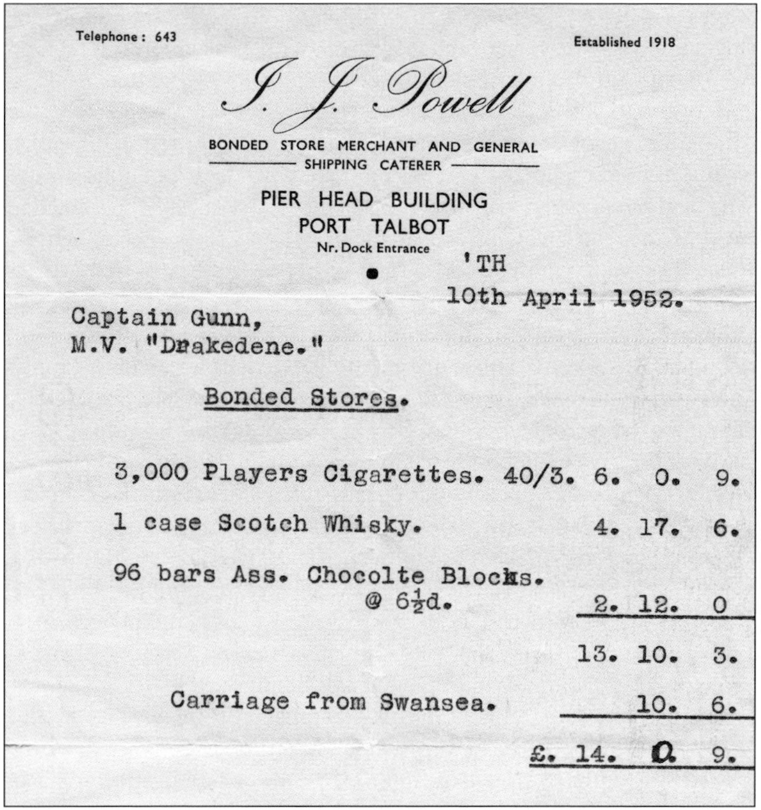
Telephone : 643

Established 1918

J. J. Powell

BONDED STORE MERCHANT AND GENERAL SHIPPING CATERER

PIER HEAD BUILDING
PORT TALBOT
Nr. Dock Entrance

'TH
10th April 1952.

Captain Gunn,
M.V. "Drakedene."

Bonded Stores.

3,000 Players Cigarettes. 40/3.	6.	0.	9.
1 case Scotch Whisky.	4.	17.	6.
96 bars Ass. Chocolte Blocks. @ 6½d.	2.	12.	0
	13.	10.	3.
Carriage from Swansea.		10.	6.
	£. 14.	0	9.

Drakedene’s Bonded Stores.

to get to Liverpool without me. By the time I went back aboard she had been fully loaded by the Mate and moved over to a lay-by berth, waiting to sail with the next tide. I packed my bags, went home to Bristol to my own ship, sold the watches to my shipmates and waited for the outcome. That took quite a long time and I was on *Ravenswood* at Newport before I received a letter saying I owed the Cardiff man money. The watches had cost more than my outstanding wages. I went to see Lyne & Co., solicitors in Newport. They knew this shipowner very well and had dealt with him before on several occasions with a similar outcome. For a £5 fee Mr Lyne undertook to sort it out to my advantage. He did and it was agreed to split the difference. Thanks to the Ghent Agent I was well covered in the end.

But it wasn't quite the end. A couple of years later I met the master who had been called out after I had left in Swansea. The ship had been overloaded on its arrival at Liverpool and he had been heavily fined. The Mate who had loaded her in my absence had been Master himself and demoted for reasons which were never discussed but easy to imagine. That captain had sailed their ships and knew them well, and once was weatherbound for more than a week close in to Lundy. Having had no word from the ship the owner was heard jubilantly saying on the telephone, 'She's gone! She's gone!' But she wasn't.

Working in London for Bolton Shipping Company was a worthwhile and enjoyable experience. British ships, like many others, were heading for a maritime depression, but our Marine Services were building up well and doing business all over the world. It was a trip to Canada to visit relatives which sent my life in a new direction. I had always wanted to live in North America and couldn't resist an offer to join two Canadians to start up a marine services business there, so I left Bolton's, and my wife and I emigrated to Toronto.

We had just started to get our own company off the ground when I was contacted by a US Group which Bolton had represented in the UK. It was another offer I couldn't refuse, as it was clearly going to take a long time to get established in Canada. My relations with GMS became strictly non-executive, and I took up an appointment to represent the US company's shipping business in Canada and the Great Lakes. There was an office already set up for me in downtown Toronto. A starting salary of $30,000 a year, a car, an expense account and air travel made the appointment even more attractive. To compete successfully in that type of business in North America, travel by air wasn't a luxury, of course, it was a necessity.

Although I had looked after their business in the UK, my first visit to the Company's headquarters in Baltimore was encouraging and very instructive. There was a lot more to be learned than I had ever realised while I had been working for them in London. There were real differences between servicing deep-sea and inland waterway vessels. I found it quite fascinating. It was the first time I had been in Baltimore since my time on the *Baron Renfrew* in 1942, and it had changed considerably. For nostalgic reasons I asked to be put up in an hotel downtown but found when I got there it was unsafe to go out. The company moved me the following day. My nostalgia had evaporated.

After having suffered the hassle of housebuying in the UK on several occasions, in Ontario such procedures were simple by comparison, quick and efficient. It took just a few days to find exactly what we wanted, and we met the owner for the first time on a Monday morning for a short discussion about the property. We arranged to meet again after lunch. Simultaneously we handed each other notes. His showed the least he was prepared to accept, ours the most that we intended to pay. They were both the same. At the time there was a postal strike so we used the same solicitor. It took just thirty minutes and a fee of $15 to re-register the property and we moved in that week.

Montreal was the obvious place to start work. I had been there only once before, when we had met in January to set up GMS. By now it was July, and the weather conditions were very different. From the outset I liked Montreal and it was always a pleasure, whatever the time of year, to work there.

It didn't take long to realise that to get the best out of any business in Quebec Province where personal contacts are required, it was necessary to speak French, preferably Quebecois. French separatism was intensifying, and was even then having effect on the lives and work of many non-French residents, including some who had been born and brought up there by British parents. The contentious issue that had never been resolved was the question of whether Britain had taken the Province from France, or France had taken it from Britain.

The only things I excelled at in school were football and French. I didn't like French but for some unaccountable reason it was easy enough to learn and I now managed to learn sufficient local French to talk about ships and their problems.

Working with passenger ferries which sailed from Dover to Calais and Zeebrugge had made me realise the importance of being able to understand what foreigners were talking about. I took the opportunity to speak to any unwitting French national whenever possible. Often I couldn't convince myself, and didn't seem to impress them, because they always broke into English which was invariably better than my French.

I had worked for Americans before emigrating to Canada and had a good idea that doing business for them was different. There wasn't the same obsession with working nine to five: what mattered were results. The time of day or night when they were obtained was immaterial. It suited someone like me, who had never worked regular hours. In North America there were always plenty of interesting challenges and much tough opposition to contend with, but I felt that in Quebec Province my ability to use French when required would be an important business asset.

Shipping on the Great Lakes was divided between USA and Canadian ownership. To a newcomer the number of vessels, their size and the economical and effective way in which they were operated, was quite remarkable. One of the main features of a bulk-carrying Laker was the ability to discharge thousands of tons of cargo completely unaided from ashore. The largest ships on the Lakes were 1000 feet long, could carry up to 80,000 tons of ore, and were fitted with self-unloading booms reaching out as far as 300 feet. They were also used to land crew members ashore to moor the vessels. Tying up, letting go, and discharging these large Lakers was in every way a self-contained operation. They were all built at shipyards on the Great Lakes and were permanently landlocked. The majority of vessels sailing on the Lakes did not conform to the specifications required for 'outside trading'; although when the War started it was amazing how quickly sufficient strengthening could be made to Canadian Lakers to enable them to sail in North Atlantic convoys to the UK and help to 'keep the door open' until the large building programme of Canadian 'Fort Boats' took effect.

The five years I spent working on the Great Lakes was a welcome addition to a varied and exciting career, and certainly one I had never considered. Like many other deep-sea men who didn't know any better, I thought sailing around inland waterways in pleasant, benign, seasonal weather conditions was an easy way to make a living 'without getting your feet wet'. It didn't take long to realise that was a complete misconception. Over the years Great Lakes seamen and their ships have had to contend with extreme conditions every bit as tough as those experienced by their foreign-going counterparts.

The trial-and-error system of ship construction which has prevailed throughout maritime history was especially prevalent on the Great Lakes and resulted in the loss of countless ships, crews and passengers. Hundreds of ship losses have been identified, but many others sunk without trace. The North American and Canadian Great Lakes have had their fair share of maritime tragedy. The Great Lakes never were, and never will be, 'a benign place to sail about in'.

One of the early reasons for shipping on the Great Lakes was to transport settlers and their families with their sparse belongings part of the way towards the 'Promised Lands' of North America. Traversing the Lakes should have been one of the least gruelling sections of their long journeys but it often proved to be the most hazardous. Some of the boat trips started in Canada, but most of the travellers embarked at the Port of Buffalo for the long haul across Lakes Erie, Huron, and on to the Western shores of Lake Superior. The passage across Superior by steamship was first made possible in 1845 when an enterprising Englishman living in Chicago decided to build a paddle-steamer (called a 'sidewheeler' in America) to carry cargo between North America and England.

After just one trip across the Atlantic fully loaded with cargo and sufficient bunker fuel for the 3000-mile crossing the entrepreneur discovered that the ship could do no more than about four knots in that condition. In order to make any reasonable speed she could just carry part cargo. That was when the Chicago man decided to try his luck on Lake Superior.

Large Bulk Carriers on the Great Lakes.

Selkirk Settler
Canadian – Gross Tons 21,549
Length 730 ft.

Belle River
USA – Gross Tons 35,923
Length 1,000 ft.

There was one major problem: how to get a large steamship into the lake. There was no navigable channel between Huron and Superior, only a river with rapids, used by trappers and Indians in canoes. The redoubtable Mr. Averill, who had heard of fortunes to be made on Lake Superior, didn't give up and decided to move his ship overland where necessary. Portage was a method of transport adopted by Indians and frontiersmen but it had certainly not been developed to haul anything like the size of SS *Independence*, which weighed more than 160 tons.

After much preparation and some alterations to the ship, including conversion from single screw to twin screw, *Independence* arrived at Sault Ste. Marie and was made ready to bypass the St. Mary river. Using wooden rollers, a sturdy crew and live horsepower, the ship was moved a mile overland between Huron and Superior in seven days and was launched into the Lake, where she traded until 1853 carrying ore, passengers, and all kinds of general cargo. Towards the end of that season, and shortly after leaving port for her last sailing of the year, the Master of the *Independence* rang 'full speed ahead' on the engine-room telegraph, the boiler exploded and the vessel was blown to bits. The first steamship to sail on Lake Superior had worked there for eight years, during which time fur trading, ore mining and passenger traffic had developed considerably.

Two years after the destruction of *Independence* the first lock was built at Sault Ste. Marie (familiarly known as 'the Soo') allowing vessels to transit between the lakes. Since then, the Soo has become the busiest locking system in the world, and can now handle the very largest vessels at some speed, by locking them through in both directions at the same time.

Hundreds of other vessels came to grief after *Independence*, with the loss of many lives. A Great Lakes story wouldn't be complete without further reference to some of the achievements and disasters which took place on these inland waterways which few in this Country know anything about. It was clear early on that to be accepted and earn a good living in North America, Canadian citizenship was a priority: there were many limitations and restrictions for 'Landed Emigrants'. A minimum of three years' residence is required. After the statutory three years we were assessed by a judge as suitable and were accepted for initiation. It was an unforgettable ceremony in Oshawa Courthouse, conducted by the judge and flanked by red-coated Mounted Police (without horses). Eighty-five of us took the Oath of Allegiance, sang the National Anthem and became certificated Canadians. There were more than twenty different nationalities present: my wife and I were the only Britons.

Our citizenship gave us full voting rights, and we used them to our advantage by joining a political party which was dedicated to getting rid of Pierre Elliot Trudeau, who had been Prime Minister for over fifteen years. Because of the many invitations I received to social occasions, I became involved in politics for the first time in my life. As Trudeau had grossly insulted the Queen on her visit to the Montreal Games, that was another good reason to join the Opposition.

Although Canadian Government seemed to represent a mixture of British and American tendencies, there was one important aspect which differed from both: informality. With the probable exception of Pierre, it was first names all round. My adopted Party won the Federal Election and disposed of Trudeau, then took the next Provincial Election at which for services rendered I was appointed a Deputy Returning Officer.

Compared with the UK and Greece, there were long distances to travel in Canada for meetings with shipping companies and perhaps that is one of the reasons they hadn't yet had the success they deserved. It made sense to cut down the travelling distances and appoint agencies in strategic places. It didn't take long to set one up in Montreal on the St Lawrence, Sarnia at the entrance to Lake Huron and at Halifax, Nova Scotia. It was a good start and gave me the best facilities possible under the circumstances. Although some US Great Lakes ships were based at Buffalo and Chicago, the main centre was Cleveland, Ohio, which was just one hour's flight from Toronto, where, as in Montreal, one visit took several days, usually from Monday to Friday.

Great Lakes, Bulkcarrying Self-Unloader, showing discharging boom which can unload all the cargo without any 'shore' assistance.

Great Lakes Bulk Carrier.

The Port and City of Cleveland fronts onto Lake Erie and stands on the Cuyahoga River, the only river ever known to be so polluted that it actually caught fire. I did a lot of work on Lakers through regular contact with the owners in Cleveland. It did help a bit being employed by an American company. When I was there, downtown Cleveland had the same 'no-go' problems as Baltimore at night, but as with every other problem there was a solution. For dinner most evenings I left the hotel car park and drove all of 400 yards to the 'Theatrical' pub/restaurant, parked right outside the front door and spent a pleasant evening knowing that I was in the safest place in Cleveland. It was owned by the Mafia and a very strict code of behaviour was always observed by patrons. This code applied particularly to females on their own who were not allowed past the big man in evening dress who guarded the door unless he personally knew exactly who they were. I took my wife there; she was very impressed with the choice and enjoyed every minute of our night out. I didn't mention who the owners were until after we had left.

In 1984 (excluding ferries) there were more than 300 vessels sailing the Lakes. A hundred of them were large, self-unloading bulk carriers up to 1000 feet long and 100 feet beam, capable of carrying up to 80,000 tons of ore. Because of the freshwater conditions in which the ships worked and laid up during the winter, there were few rust problems, which was, of course, very different from deep-sea vessels operating out in the Atlantic. My self-taught expertise in corrosion control was surplus to requirements when servicing Lakers. Most of the work was cosmetic, but vessels had to be painted well enough in the spring to maintain a smart appearance for a nine-month trading season until winter closed in and the locks closed down. Most of my work on board the Lakers took place out of season when they were mainly laid up at shipyard ports for repairs and refits. Driving long distances in Canada and USA was an important part of the job, and it was a good way to see parts of North America I'd never even heard about and which I am unlikely to forget. Starting up in North America was a lot easier than expected: as in Greece, personal contacts were essential and a British background in shipping reaped its rewards.

With their good shipbuilding and drydocking facilities, the main ports I worked in outside the Lakes were Montreal, Quebec and Halifax, where on one occasion I attended two ships at the same time, one in Collingwood, Ontario, and the other in Halifax, Nova Scotia. As the superintendent said at the time, 'You can do it, George, they're not very far from each other.' Only 1500 miles. In Canada the term 'just up the road' has a different meaning than it would have in the UK, but 1500 miles was a bit excessive even for them.

I did quite a lot of work at that time for Q&O, the owners of a fleet of ships trading in and outside the Lakes. A rather unusual job was to try and get one of their vessels into a presentable enough condition for sale. Without seeing the ship I took up the challenge; she was laid up in the Port of Sorel about 50 miles east of Montreal and 120 miles west of Quebec City.

Baie Comeau is a seaport in Quebec Province. *Baie Comeau 2* was a ship owned by Q&O Transportation in Ontario and named after the port from which she regularly traded to Florida and other US seaports. The owners wanted the ship sold and so did the 12,000 townspeople of Baie Comeau, as they felt their good name was being sullied by the vessel's rusty appearance. I was asked by the ship's manager to do what I could to make her attractive to prospective buyers. The Mate in charge had a problem on his hands, as the men sent from the Seaman's Pool would only speak French and took advantage of that to do as little work as possible. Unfortunately he didn't know enough of the language to do much about it. The shipping recession was well under way elsewhere and had spread as far as Canada, and the men were using whatever tactics they could to make the job last as long as possible.

My hotel in Sorel was conveniently close to the ship and during the day I made full use of the Captain's cabin. From the masts down to the waterline, including all the superstructure and hull, the ship was in a mess and I could understand why the good people of Baie Comeau had renounced any connection with it.

My first day there got off to a fairly good start. I arrived from Toronto at lunchtime, joined the crew in a cafe and bought a couple of

Baie Comeau 2 at Sorel for refurbishment. By that time we had managed to renovate the bridge, but clearly there was still a long way to go.

carafes of vin rouge. They seemed to understand my French all right when I asked what they would like to drink. One answered in English and I immediately put him in charge, gave him the keys of the store locker and made him responsible for issuing and looking after the equipment for the work. According to the inventory, the incidence of chipping hammers, wire brushes and paint scrapers dropped down into the dock thereafter decreased considerably.

After ten days, which included a weekend at home in Toronto, work on *Baie Comeau* was completed. Underneath all the rust and old paint blisters we found quite a good ship, and as the engines were in working order the vessel seemed to be in a good condition for sale – at least to the Greeks. Getting a good result after working for ten days with a crew of French-only speaking sailors on a ship like that, in a place like Sorel in the heat of summer, was quite satisfying. The owners put it like this: '*Baie Comeau* was back in her best livery and would be sold to foreign buyers'. I thought that description was a bit over the top.

A group of New York businessmen were interested in purchasing a suitable vessel to sail between New York City and Atlantic City carrying clients for hotels and casinos. By arrangement with the hotels and casinos in Atlantic City, very cheap (and in some cases free) accommodation would be provided for a punter's stay. All that was needed was the right ship for the job. A shipbroker colleague asked me to inspect one of the large Lake Michigan ferries which carried vehicles, passengers and railcars across the Lake between Michigan and Wisconsin. It was on a route I usually took from Toronto to the shipyards in Sturgeon Bay. That round trip was about 1000 miles. Both ferries were for sale. *Spartan* was still in service and the other one was laid up at Ludington, so I had the opportunity to look at each ship very thoroughly under different circumstances. Considering their age they were both in excellent condition, and from the set of *Spartan* drawings with which I was provided either of the ships would have been suitable.

While I was at Bay Shipbuilders at Sturgeon Bay attending two Lakers which were being fitted with self-unloading equipment, there was much interest and enthusiasm at the prospect of getting the work on *Spartan*, but not sufficient to submit an acceptable tender. Having spent so much time on the ship I was disappointed at the outcome.

Despite the distance to get there it was always a pleasure to go to Sturgeon Bay and sail across Lake Michigan on *Spartan* from Ludington and Keewaunee. On one occasion the return trip to Ludington was cancelled owing to bad weather, as was the next one twenty-four hours later. I was advised by the barman in what looked like the best place in town, to drive round to Green Bay rather than stay in Keewaunee. To satisfy my curiosity I mentioned the sign on the outskirts of the town which read 'WELCOME TO KEEWAUNEE Pop. 2002', and asked how that could ever be correct. He said, 'Well, when a gal gets pregnant at least one guy leaves town.'

I spent one night in Green Bay and stayed in a very comfortable hotel which was frequented on this occasion by the Master and officers of one of the Lykes Line vessels registered in New Orleans.

During what was an extremely sociable evening I agreed to visit the ship the following morning to have a look at some of the vessel's corrosion problems. Lykes' fleet of ships traded all over the world and they were one of the major clients of the company with whom I was associated. It was the first and last time I worked in Green Bay but it is likely that, unless anyone in the UK happened to see the film featuring the Green Bay Packers football team and their famous coach, Knute Rockne, they wouldn't know where it was either.

Oshawa, where our Citizenship Ceremony took place, was a seaport in its own right. It was ten miles east of where I lived and 330 miles west of Montreal. Situated on Lake Ontario, it was the first port that vessels would pass on their way to Toronto and up the Seaway. It could take a long time to discharge in Montreal, and in Toronto it was considered expensive, so I was asked by the Montreal agents to look after some of their ships for them if they decided that they should berth in Oshawa instead to unload their cargoes. There were several advantages to accepting the job: Oshawa was close to where I lived, and it was mutually very beneficial financially. Finally, another interesting challenge had arisen: to get the ships in and out quicker than anywhere else.

The vessels we berthed at Oshawa arrived there from Spain via Montreal to discharge the remainder of their steel cargo before heading up the Lakes to load for Europe. A photograph of *Maria Lemos* (opposite) shows her arriving at Oshawa after battling gale force winds and heavy seas right across the North Atlantic. Three weeks of rolling around with a full cargo of steel lying in the bottom of the holds of a small cargo ship in the Western Ocean was a very uncomfortable experience.

Maria Lemos was the first of a number of similar vessels I attended to, and despite the state of that ship, I started to feel that it was time to get back on the bridge again after having spent more than thirty years doing little else but handle ships. There was, of course, a major problem: to take charge of a Canadian-registered vessel required a Canadian Master's licence. The Coastguards who conducted the examinations and issued the licences suggested I had a go. It was

Maria Lemos arriving Oshawa: the cargo of coal in the background had been discharged during the night from the Self-Unloader.

DEPARTMENT OF TRANSPORT
BY THE HONOURABLE THE MINISTER OF TRANSPORT

CANADA

MINISTÈRE DES TRANSPORTS
PAR L'HONORABLE MINISTRE DES TRANSPORTS

CERTIFICATE OF COMPETENCY
as
FIRST MATE of a FOREIGN-Going steamship or MASTER of a Home-Trade or Inland Waters Steamship.

CERTIFICAT DE CAPACITÉ
de
PREMIER LIEUTENANT de navire à vapeur au long cours ou de CAPITAINE de navire à vapeur au cabotage ou d'eaux intérieures.

GEORGE SMITH GUNN

WHEREAS it has been reported to me that you have been found duly qualified to fulfil the duties of First Mate of a Foreign-Going Steamship or Master of a Home-Trade or Inland Waters Steamship, I do hereby in pursuance of the Canada Shipping Act, grant you this Certificate of Competency.

VU le rapport attestant votre aptitude à exercer les fonctions de Premier Lieutenant de navire à vapeur au long cours ou de Capitaine de navire à vapeur au cabotage ou d'eaux intérieures, je vous délivre le présent certificat de capacité conformément aux dispositions de la Loi sur la marine marchande du Canada.

GIVEN under the SEAL OF THE MINISTER OF TRANSPORT at OTTAWA.

DONNÉ sous le SCEAU DU MINISTRE DES TRANSPORTS à OTTAWA.

Registered — *Enregistré*

L. H. Vermeersch
(for) Minister of Transport — *(pour le) Ministre des Transports*

Date of Birth — *Date de naissance*	Date of Issue — *Date de délivrance*	~~Date of Expiry — Date d'expiration~~
8.6.23	28.2.85	

Signature of Holder — *Signature du titulaire*	Certificate No. — *Certificat n^o^*
	ON1- 85-07032

82-0603

My Canadian Master's Licence.

many years since I had sat for my Master's Certificate in Britain, but I took up the challenge and spent most of my spare time studying. My work as a part-time ship's agent at Oshawa fitted in well and I passed for a Canadian Master's Licence in 1985.

The Ontario Government in the meantime produced plans for an extensive development of the Port of Oshawa, and just at that time the Harbour Master decided to retire. I was invited to apply for the job. It was a Government appointment and as the Conservatives were in power, everything looked good, since I was an active member of the Party and well enough known in the area. However, disaster struck. There was an election which the Liberals won and I lost. The Harbour Master's secretary got the job without having any marine qualifications or practical experience in the business. The lady had the right connections: she was a Liberal. We were in fact planning to return to the UK when the pound/dollar exchange rate hit the right level. That took some time and I joined a small passenger ship as Master and had a wonderful time sailing around Lake Ontario, the St Lawrence River and the picturesque Thousand Islands.

The *Island Queen* was different from any ship I had ever sailed on, or indeed been aboard: it was a showboat with built-in entertainment. In addition to wonderful scenic cruises on Lake Ontario, up and down the St. Lawrence river and through the Thousand Islands, we provided a full range of variety entertainment. *Island Queen* was the Mississippi showboat of the St. Lawrence, great fun for the countless visitors who sailed on the ship, and even for a captain who handled her. Down below she had two powerful Volvo marine engines and a chief engineer who had been with the vessel since the first day she came into service more than nine years previously. It was an unbeatable combination and sometimes a source of wonderment to passengers when they watched the puny little imitation stern wheel turning in accordance with the ship's movements through the water. The bearings of that wheel had to be kept well lubricated, as we didn't wish to mislead any of our passengers, but neither did we want to disappoint them.

The little vessel could do ten knots, was built entirely of

Island Queen. Saturday Wedding Party at Kingston, Ontario.

aluminum, and was licensed to carry up to 300 passengers. She did three regular three-hour cruises a day from May through to November, with frequent evening charters and a few night-time 'gigs'. There were excellent bar and dining facilities on board, but on night-time cruises and gigs we had to exercise discreet but rigorous control over alcohol consumption. Residents of Ontario weren't unused to drinking restrictions, and what was accepted but perhaps not liked there, wouldn't have been tolerated in the UK even in 1986. Anyone looking the worse for wear was refused entry. Nobody was allowed to bring any alcoholic drink on board. Women never refused to open their handbags for inspection, and even if they disliked the idea, men seldom objected to being 'frisked'. At the gangway they had to get past our security man, the chief engineer, who was a Jamaican weightlifting champion with very obvious credentials.

St. Lawrence River: the island on the left is in Canada, and the island on the right is in the United States.

St. Lawrence River: Boldt Castle, where the chef invented the famous Thousand Island salad-dressing.

The decision on whether to stay permanently in Canada had to be made, as the dollar/pound situation seemed to be getting more favourable. To obtain the best of both worlds it would be ideal to live and work in Canada for the summer and stay in the UK during the winter. The working association with *Island Queen* had been very successful all round and I had the option of sailing the ship for the summer seasons and living in the UK during the winter. There was no problem with having the right accommodation at both ends: we already had a deposit on a new house to be built in Swansea, just a few hundred yards away from the one we had sold when we left there thirteen years previously.

Financially, working for a seven-month period in Canada was the equivalent of a full year in Britain. That perfect arrangement was agreed. However, after settling down at home in the new house for six months we became increasingly reluctant to keep flying back and forward across the Atlantic, whatever the benefits. Although the agreement was suspended for the first year, and still available after that, we settled down back in Swansea as though we had never left the place. Winning a couple of local government elections and getting politically involved again was another challenging and interesting part of my life, and I shall always be grateful for the pleasure I had from the six years I subsequently spent as a Swansea City and a West Glamorgan County Councillor, and for the many friends I made and colleagues, whatever party they represented, with whom I worked during that time. Now that I have retired at last I have plenty of time on my hands to write about such experiences, and perhaps that will be my next challenge.

Appendix 1: Tramping as it was

A question sometimes asked is, 'What was a tramp steamer? Was it the way a ship looked or what it did?' The answer is probably a little of both. The description fitted the majority of pre-war vessels sailing 'foreign' out of UK ports. A poem written by a member of the crew on one of my old ships, *Baron Yarborough*, explains it more precisely:

Trampship

Four thousand tons in battered steel,
tempered by storm from truck to keel,
Bearing scars received worldwide,
patches of rust along her side;
In need of paint, no gracious maiden,
she plows her way deeply laden,
Bluff of bow, broad of beam,
she tramps the oceans driven by steam;
Square bridge weathered by driven spray,
keeps constant lookout night and day,
Soot caked funnel, woodwork bleached by salt,
constant journey knows little halt.
Not built for beauty nor for play,
just a working seahorse, that's her way,
Holds crammed full with God knows what,
haul anything anywhere, that's her lot;
Maybe general cargo or holds filled with coal,
maybe locos on deck, 'God how she'll roll,'
Maybe iron ore, timber, phosphates, or grain,
anything anywhere, it's all the same.
Not for her a regular run,
she goes wherever deals are done,
Plunging foc's'tle reeling masts,
through endless distance her voyage lasts.
You can't sign on her for a three-week trip,
She's away for ever, an old tramp's ship.

Ken Sherrocks

APPENDIX 2: SS *Sheaf Holme* & The Longest Voyage

My first trip to sea as an apprentice must have seemed a very short one to our Third Mate, Nelson K. Harvey, when the ship arrived back in Hull in March 1942 after a voyage of only seven months. My next trip on the same ship was a round-the-world voyage on which we sailed an estimated 47,360 miles in twelve months.

I didn't know then of Nelson's first trip to sea, which started in Hartlepool on 13th August 1933, and ended in Sunderland on 20th February 1938 – probably the longest trampship voyage in history.

There are a number of definite reasons for which a boy goes to sea, one being that he has no ambition to do anything else. Nelson was one of those, and despite trying very hard to get away as an apprentice or cadet with a shipping company, he had to make the best job of being assistant projectionist in the local picture-house. However, perseverance told in the end, and he couldn't believe his luck when a telegram arrived from W. A. Souter & Company of Newcastle offering him an apprenticeship on their motor vessel, *Sheaf Holme*. Nelson's film career ended abruptly and he lost no time in joining the ship.

The crew had been informed that the ship was going for a fairly short trip to the States and back, but that misinformation was routine on the old sailing vessels and their successors in world trade tramping. Old hands usually took it with a pinch of salt. Although it was nice to get home after a voyage, it was also nice to get away to sea again, irrespective of living conditions on board some ships. Unless a seaman stayed with a ship until it reached a UK/Continent port, the only chance of getting home was from serious injury or illness and only then if certified as DBS (Distressed British Seaman). The company's responsibility and the man's wages ceased when he left the ship, even if it was in a lifeboat or on a life-raft. Any seamen's union around at the time went unrecognised ashore and afloat and was tolerated rather than acknowledged. It was all just part of a 'real man's life'.

Sheaf Holme 'listing' her way on the long passage across the Pacific with a deck cargo of timber from Vancouver.